THE ENCYCLICALS OF BENEDICT XVI

BY
POPE BENEDICT XVI

*All booklets are published thanks to the generous support
of the members of the Catholic Truth Society*

CATHOLIC TRUTH SOCIETY
PUBLISHERS TO THE HOLY SEE

CTS Publications

CTS booklets explain the faith, teaching and life of the Catholic Church. They are based on Sacred Scripture, the Second Vatican Council documents, and the Catechism of the Catholic Church. Our booklets provide authentic Catholic teaching; they address issues of life and of truth which are relevant to all. They aim to inform and educate readers on the many issues that people have to deal with today.

In addition, CTS nurtures and supports the Christian life through its many spiritual, liturgical, educational and pastoral books. As Publisher to the Holy See, CTS publishes the official documents of the Catholic Church as they are issued.

website: CTSbooks.org

First Edition published 2013 by The Incorporated Catholic Truth Society 40-46 Harleyford Road London SE11 5AY Tel: 020 7640 0042 Fax: 020 7640 0046. **Deus Caritas Est***: Copyright © 2006 Libreria Editrice Vaticana, Citta del Vaticano. This edition © 2006, 2013 The Incorporated Catholic Truth Society.* **Spe Salvi***: Copyright © 2007 Libreria Editrice Vaticana, Citta del Vaticano. This edition © 2007, 2013 The Incorporated Catholic Truth Society.* **Caritas in Veritate***: Copyright © 2009 Libreria Editrice Vaticana, Citta del Vaticano. This edition © 2009, 2013 The Incorporated Catholic Truth Society.*

ISBN 978 1 86082 864 5

Front Cover Image: Benedict XVI, Visit to Great Britain 2010 © *Stefano Spaziani.*

CONTENTS

ENCYCLICAL LETTER

Deus Caritas Est

OF THE SUPREME PONTIFF

BENEDICT XVI

TO THE BISHOPS
PRIESTS AND DEACONS
MEN AND WOMEN RELIGIOUS
AND ALL THE LAY FAITHFUL

ON CHRISTIAN LOVE

CONTENTS

INTRODUCTION

1. "God is love, and he who abides in love abides in God, and God abides in him" (*1 Jn* 4:16). These words from the *First Letter of John* express with remarkable clarity the heart of the Christian faith: the Christian image of God and the resulting image of mankind and its destiny. In the same verse, Saint John also offers a kind of summary of the Christian life: "We have come to know and to believe in the love God has for us".

We have come to believe in God's love: in these words the Christian can express the fundamental decision of his life. Being Christian is not the result of an ethical choice or a lofty idea, but the encounter with an event, a person, which gives life a new horizon and a decisive direction. Saint John's Gospel describes that event in these words: "God so loved the world that he gave his only Son, that whoever believes in him should...have eternal life" (3:16). In acknowledging the centrality of love, Christian faith has retained the core of Israel's faith, while at the same time giving it new depth and breadth. The pious Jew prayed daily the words of the *Book of Deuteronomy* which expressed the heart of his existence: "Hear, O Israel: the Lord our God is one Lord, and you shall love the Lord your God with all your heart, and with all your soul and with all your might" (6:4-5). Jesus united into a single precept this commandment of love for God and the commandment of love for neighbour found in the *Book of Leviticus*: "You shall love your neighbour as yourself" (19:18; cf. *Mk* 12:29-31). Since God has first loved us (cf. *1 Jn* 4:10), love is now no longer a mere "command"; it is the response to the gift of love with which God draws near to us.

In a world where the name of God is sometimes associated with vengeance or even a duty of hatred and violence, this message is both timely and significant. For this reason, I wish in my first Encyclical to speak of the love which God lavishes upon us and which we in turn must share with others. That, in essence, is what the two main parts of this Letter are about, and they are profoundly interconnected. The first part is more speculative, since I wanted here - at the beginning of my Pontificate - to clarify some essential facts concerning the love which God mysteriously and gratuitously offers to man, together with the intrinsic link between that Love and the reality of human love. The second part is more concrete, since it treats the ecclesial exercise of the commandment of love of neighbour. The argument has vast implications, but a lengthy treatment would go beyond the scope of the present Encyclical. I wish to emphasise some basic elements, so as to call forth in the world renewed energy and commitment in the human response to God's love.

PART I

THE UNITY OF LOVE IN CREATION AND IN SALVATION HISTORY

A problem of language

2. God's love for us is fundamental for our lives, and it raises important questions about who God is and who we are. In considering this, we immediately find ourselves hampered by a problem of language. Today, the term "love" has become one of the most frequently used and misused of words, a word to which we attach quite different meanings. Even though this Encyclical will deal primarily with the understanding and practice of love in sacred Scripture and in the Church's Tradition, we cannot simply prescind from the meaning of the word in the different cultures and in present-day usage.

Let us first of all bring to mind the vast semantic range of the word "love": we speak of love of country, love of one's profession, love between friends, love of work, love between parents and children, love between family members, love of neighbour and love of God. Amid this multiplicity of meanings, however, one in particular stands out: love between man and woman, where body and soul are inseparably joined and human beings glimpse an apparently irresistible promise of happiness. This would seem to be the very epitome of love; all other kinds of love immediately seem to fade in comparison. So we need to ask: are all these forms of love basically one, so that love, in its many and varied manifestations, is ultimately a single reality, or are we merely using the same word to designate totally different realities?

"Eros" and "Agape" - difference and unity

3. That love between man and woman which is neither planned nor willed, but somehow imposes itself upon human beings, was called *eros* by the ancient Greeks. Let us note straight away that the Greek

Old Testament uses the word *eros* only twice, while the New Testament does not use it at all: of the three Greek words for love, *eros*, *philia* (the love of friendship) and *agape*, New Testament writers prefer the last, which occurs rather infrequently in Greek usage. As for the term *philia*, the love of friendship, it is used with added depth of meaning in Saint John's Gospel in order to express the relationship between Jesus and his disciples. The tendency to avoid the word *eros*, together with the new vision of love expressed through the word *agape*, clearly point to something new and distinct about the Christian understanding of love. In the critique of Christianity which began with the Enlightenment and grew progressively more radical, this new element was seen as something thoroughly negative. According to Friedrich Nietzsche, Christianity had poisoned *eros*, which for its part, while not completely succumbing, gradually degenerated into vice.[1] Here the German philosopher was expressing a widely-held perception: doesn't the Church, with all her commandments and prohibitions, turn to bitterness the most precious thing in life? Doesn't she blow the whistle just when the joy which is the Creator's gift offers us a happiness which is itself a certain foretaste of the Divine?

4. But is this the case? Did Christianity really destroy *eros*? Let us take a look at the pre-Christian world. The Greeks - not unlike other cultures - considered *eros* principally as a kind of intoxication, the overpowering of reason by a "divine madness" which tears man away from his finite existence and enables him, in the very process of being overwhelmed by divine power, to experience supreme happiness. All other powers in heaven and on earth thus appear secondary: "*Omnia vincit amor*" says Virgil in the *Bucolics* - love conquers all - and he adds: "*et nos cedamus amori*" - let us, too, yield to love.[2] In the religions, this attitude found expression in fertility cults, part of which was the "sacred" prostitution which

[1] Cf. *Jenseits von Gut und Böse*, IV, 168.
[2] X, 69.

flourished in many temples. *Eros* was thus celebrated as divine power, as fellowship with the Divine.

The Old Testament firmly opposed this form of religion, which represents a powerful temptation against monotheistic faith, combating it as a perversion of religiosity. But it in no way rejected *eros* as such; rather, it declared war on a warped and destructive form of it, because this counterfeit divinisation of *eros* actually strips it of its dignity and dehumanises it. Indeed, the prostitutes in the temple, who had to bestow this divine intoxication, were not treated as human beings and persons, but simply used as a means of arousing "divine madness": far from being goddesses, they were human persons being exploited. An intoxicated and undisciplined *eros*, then, is not an ascent in "ecstasy" towards the Divine, but a fall, a degradation of man. Evidently, *eros* needs to be disciplined and purified if it is to provide not just fleeting pleasure, but a certain foretaste of the pinnacle of our existence, of that beatitude for which our whole being yearns.

5. Two things emerge clearly from this rapid overview of the concept of *eros* past and present. First, there is a certain relationship between love and the Divine: love promises infinity, eternity - a reality far greater and totally other than our everyday existence. Yet we have also seen that the way to attain this goal is not simply by submitting to instinct. Purification and growth in maturity are called for; and these also pass through the path of renunciation. Far from rejecting or "poisoning" *eros*, they heal it and restore its true grandeur.

This is due first and foremost to the fact that man is a being made up of body and soul. Man is truly himself when his body and soul are intimately united; the challenge of *eros* can be said to be truly overcome when this unification is achieved. Should he aspire to be pure spirit and to reject the flesh as pertaining to his animal nature alone, then spirit and body would both lose their dignity. On the other hand, should he deny the spirit and consider matter, the body, as the only reality, he would likewise lose his greatness. The epicure

Gassendi used to offer Descartes the humorous greeting: "O Soul!" And Descartes would reply: "O Flesh!"[3] Yet it is neither the spirit alone nor the body alone that loves: it is man, the person, a unified creature composed of body and soul, who loves. Only when both dimensions are truly united, does man attain his full stature. Only thus is love - *eros* - able to mature and attain its authentic grandeur.

Nowadays Christianity of the past is often criticised as having been opposed to the body; and it is quite true that tendencies of this sort have always existed. Yet the contemporary way of exalting the body is deceptive. *Eros*, reduced to pure "sex", has become a commodity, a mere "thing" to be bought and sold, or rather, man himself becomes a commodity. This is hardly man's great "yes" to the body. On the contrary, he now considers his body and his sexuality as the purely material part of himself, to be used and exploited at will. Nor does he see it as an arena for the exercise of his freedom, but as a mere object that he attempts, as he pleases, to make both enjoyable and harmless. Here we are actually dealing with a debasement of the human body: no longer is it integrated into our overall existential freedom; no longer is it a vital expression of our whole being, but it is more or less relegated to the purely biological sphere. The apparent exaltation of the body can quickly turn into a hatred of bodiliness. Christian faith, on the other hand, has always considered man a unity in duality, a reality in which spirit and matter compenetrate, and in which each is brought to a new nobility. True, *eros* tends to rise "in ecstasy" towards the Divine, to lead us beyond ourselves; yet for this very reason it calls for a path of ascent, renunciation, purification and healing.

6. Concretely, what does this path of ascent and purification entail? How might love be experienced so that it can fully realise its human and divine promise? Here we can find a first, important indication in the *Song of Songs*, an Old Testament book well known to the mystics. According to the interpretation generally held today, the

---

[3] Cf. R. Descartes, *Œuvres, ed. V. Cousin*, vol. 12, Paris 1824, pp. 95ff.

poems contained in this book were originally love-songs, perhaps intended for a Jewish wedding feast and meant to exalt conjugal love. In this context it is highly instructive to note that in the course of the book two different Hebrew words are used to indicate "love". First there is the word *dodim*, a plural form suggesting a love that is still insecure, indeterminate and searching. This comes to be replaced by the word *ahabà*, which the Greek version of the Old Testament translates with the similar-sounding *agape*, which, as we have seen, becomes the typical expression for the biblical notion of love. By contrast with an indeterminate, "searching" love, this word expresses the experience of a love which involves a real discovery of the other, moving beyond the selfish character that prevailed earlier. Love now becomes concern and care for the other. No longer is it self-seeking, a sinking in the intoxication of happiness; instead it seeks the good of the beloved: it becomes renunciation and it is ready, and even willing, for sacrifice.

It is part of love's growth towards higher levels and inward purification that it now seeks to become definitive, and it does so in a twofold sense: both in the sense of exclusivity (this particular person alone) and in the sense of being "for ever". Love embraces the whole of existence in each of its dimensions, including the dimension of time. It could hardly be otherwise, since its promise looks towards its definitive goal: love looks to the eternal. Love is indeed "ecstasy", not in the sense of a moment of intoxication, but rather as a journey, an ongoing exodus out of the closed inward-looking self towards its liberation through self-giving, and thus towards authentic self-discovery and indeed the discovery of God: "Whoever seeks to gain his life will lose it, but whoever loses his life will preserve it" (*Lk* 17:33), as Jesus says throughout the Gospels (cf. *Mt* 10:39; 16:25; *Mk* 8:35; *Lk* 9:24; *Jn* 12:25). In these words, Jesus portrays his own path, which leads through the Cross to the Resurrection: the path of the grain of wheat that falls to the ground and dies, and in this way bears much fruit. Starting from the depths of his own sacrifice and of the love that reaches fulfilment therein, he also portrays in these words the essence of love and indeed of human life itself.

7. By their own inner logic, these initial, somewhat philosophical reflections on the essence of love have now brought us to the threshold of biblical faith. We began by asking whether the different, or even opposed, meanings of the word "love" point to some profound underlying unity, or whether on the contrary they must remain unconnected, one alongside the other. More significantly, though, we questioned whether the message of love proclaimed to us by the Bible and the Church's Tradition has some points of contact with the common human experience of love, or whether it is opposed to that experience. This in turn led us to consider two fundamental words: *eros*, as a term to indicate "worldly" love and *agape*, referring to love grounded in and shaped by faith. The two notions are often contrasted as "ascending" love and "descending" love. There are other, similar classifications, such as the distinction between possessive love and oblative love (*amor concupiscentiae - amor benevolentiae*), to which is sometimes also added love that seeks its own advantage.

In philosophical and theological debate, these distinctions have often been radicalised to the point of establishing a clear antithesis between them: descending, oblative love - *agape* - would be typically Christian, while on the other hand ascending, possessive or covetous love - *eros* - would be typical of non-Christian, and particularly Greek culture. Were this antithesis to be taken to extremes, the essence of Christianity would be detached from the vital relations fundamental to human existence, and would become a world apart, admirable perhaps, but decisively cut off from the complex fabric of human life. Yet *eros* and *agape* - ascending love and descending love - can never be completely separated. The more the two, in their different aspects, find a proper unity in the one reality of love, the more the true nature of love in general is realised. Even if *eros* is at first mainly covetous and ascending, a fascination for the great promise of happiness, in drawing near to the other, it is less and less concerned with itself, increasingly seeks the happiness of the other, is concerned more and more with the beloved, bestows itself and wants to "be there for" the other. The element of *agape* thus enters into this love, for otherwise *eros* is impoverished and even loses its own nature. On the other hand, man cannot live by oblative, descending love alone. He cannot always give, he must also receive. Anyone who wishes to give love must also receive love as a gift. Certainly, as the Lord tells us, one can become a source from which rivers of living water flow (cf. *Jn* 7:37-38). Yet to become such a source, one must constantly drink anew from the original source, which is Jesus Christ, from whose pierced heart flows the love of God (cf. *Jn* 19:34).

In the account of Jacob's ladder, the Fathers of the Church saw this inseparable connection between ascending and descending love, between *eros* which seeks God and *agape* which passes on the gift received, symbolised in various ways. In that biblical passage we read how the Patriarch Jacob saw in a dream, above the stone which was his pillow, a ladder reaching up to heaven, on which the angels of God were ascending and descending (cf. *Gn* 28:12; *Jn* 1:51). A particularly striking interpretation of this vision is presented by Pope Gregory the Great in his *Pastoral Rule*. He tells us that the good pastor must be rooted in contemplation. Only in this way will he be able to take upon himself the needs of others and make them his own: "*per pietatis viscera in se infirmitatem caeterorum transferat*".[4] Saint Gregory speaks in this context of Saint Paul, who was borne aloft to the most exalted mysteries of God, and hence, having descended once more, he was able to become all things to all men (cf. *2 Co* 12:2-4; *1 Co* 9:22). He also points to the example of Moses, who entered the tabernacle time and again, remaining in dialogue with God, so that when he emerged he could be at the service of his people. "Within [the tent] he is borne aloft through contemplation, while without he is completely engaged in helping those who suffer: *intus in contemplationem rapitur, foris infirmantium negotiis urgetur*."[5]

---

[4] II, 5: SCh 381, 196.

[5] Ibid., 198.

8. We have thus come to an initial, albeit still somewhat generic response to the two questions raised earlier. Fundamentally, "love" is a single reality, but with different dimensions; at different times, one or other dimension may emerge more clearly. Yet when the two dimensions are totally cut off from one another, the result is a caricature or at least an impoverished form of love. And we have also seen, synthetically, that biblical faith does not set up a parallel universe, or one opposed to that primordial human phenomenon which is love, but rather accepts the whole man; it intervenes in his search for love in order to purify it and to reveal new dimensions of it. This newness of biblical faith is shown chiefly in two elements which deserve to be highlighted: the image of God and the image of man.

The newness of biblical faith

9. First, the world of the Bible presents us with a new image of God. In surrounding cultures, the image of God and of the gods ultimately remained unclear and contradictory. In the development of biblical faith, however, the content of the prayer fundamental to Israel, the *Shema*, became increasingly clear and unequivocal: "Hear, O Israel, the Lord our God is one Lord" (*Dt* 6:4). There is only one God, the Creator of heaven and earth, who is thus the God of all. Two facts are significant about this statement: all other gods are not God, and the universe in which we live has its source in God and was created by him. Certainly, the notion of creation is found elsewhere, yet only here does it become absolutely clear that it is not one god among many, but the one true God himself who is the source of all that exists; the whole world comes into existence by the power of his creative Word. Consequently, his creation is dear to him, for it was willed by him and "made" by him. The second important element now emerges: this God loves man. The divine power that Aristotle at the height of Greek philosophy sought to grasp through reflection, is indeed for every being an object of desire and of love - and as the object of love this divinity

moves the world[6] - but in itself it lacks nothing and does not love: it is solely the object of love. The one God in whom Israel believes, on the other hand, loves with a personal love. His love, moreover, is an elective love: among all the nations he chooses Israel and loves her - but he does so precisely with a view to healing the whole human race. God loves, and his love may certainly be called *eros*, yet it is also totally *agape*.[7]

The Prophets, particularly Hosea and Ezekiel, described God's passion for his people using boldly erotic images. God's relationship with Israel is described using the metaphors of betrothal and marriage; idolatry is thus adultery and prostitution. Here we find a specific reference - as we have seen - to the fertility cults and their abuse of *eros*, but also a description of the relationship of fidelity between Israel and her God. The history of the love-relationship between God and Israel consists, at the deepest level, in the fact that he gives her the *Torah*, thereby opening Israel's eyes to man's true nature and showing her the path leading to true humanism. It consists in the fact that man, through a life of fidelity to the one God, comes to experience himself as loved by God, and discovers joy in truth and in righteousness - a joy in God which becomes his essential happiness: "Whom do I have in heaven but you? And there is nothing upon earth that I desire besides you...for me it is good to be near God" (*Ps* 73 [72]:25, 28).

10. We have seen that God's *eros* for man is also totally *agape*. This is not only because it is bestowed in a completely gratuitous manner, without any previous merit, but also because it is love which forgives. Hosea above all shows us that this *agape* dimension of God's love for man goes far beyond the aspect of gratuity. Israel has committed "adultery" and has broken the covenant; God should judge and repudiate her. It is precisely at this point that God is

---

[6] Cf. *Metaphysics*, XII, 7.

[7] Cf. Ps.-Dionysius the Areopagite, who in his treatise *The Divine Names*, IV, 12-14: PG 3, 709-713 calls God both *eros* and *agape*.

revealed to be God and not man: "How can I give you up, O Ephraim! How can I hand you over, O Israel!...My heart recoils within me, my compassion grows warm and tender. I will not execute my fierce anger, I will not again destroy Ephraim; for I am God and not man, the Holy One in your midst" (*Ho* 11:8-9). God's passionate love for his people - for humanity - is at the same time a forgiving love. It is so great that it turns God against himself, his love against his justice. Here Christians can see a dim prefigurement of the mystery of the Cross: so great is God's love for man that by becoming man he follows him even into death, and so reconciles justice and love.

The philosophical dimension to be noted in this biblical vision, and its importance from the standpoint of the history of religions, lies in the fact that on the one hand we find ourselves before a strictly metaphysical image of God: God is the absolute and ultimate source of all being; but this universal principle of creation - the *Logos*, primordial reason - is at the same time a lover with all the passion of a true love. *Eros* is thus supremely ennobled, yet at the same time it is so purified as to become one with *agape*. We can thus see how the reception of the *Song of Songs* in the canon of sacred Scripture was soon explained by the idea that these love songs ultimately describe God's relation to man and man's relation to God. Thus the *Song of Songs* became, both in Christian and Jewish literature, a source of mystical knowledge and experience, an expression of the essence of biblical faith: that man can indeed enter into union with God - his primordial aspiration. But this union is no mere fusion, a sinking in the nameless ocean of the Divine; it is a unity which creates love, a unity in which both God and man remain themselves and yet become fully one. As Saint Paul says: "He who is united to the Lord becomes one spirit with him" (*1 Co* 6:17).

11. The first novelty of biblical faith consists, as we have seen, in its image of God. The second, essentially connected to this, is found in the image of man. The biblical account of creation speaks of the solitude of Adam, the first man, and God's decision to give

18

him a helper. Of all other creatures, not one is capable of being the helper that man needs, even though he has assigned a name to all the wild beasts and birds and thus made them fully a part of his life. So God forms woman from the rib of man. Now Adam finds the helper that he needed: "This at last is bone of my bones and flesh of my flesh" (*Gn* 2:23). Here one might detect hints of ideas that are also found, for example, in the myth mentioned by Plato, according to which man was originally spherical, because he was complete in himself and self-sufficient. But as a punishment for pride, he was split in two by Zeus, so that now he longs for his other half, striving with all his being to possess it and thus regain his integrity.[8] While the biblical narrative does not speak of punishment, the idea is certainly present that man is somehow incomplete, driven by nature to seek in another the part that can make him whole, the idea that only in communion with the opposite sex can he become "complete". The biblical account thus concludes with a prophecy about Adam: "Therefore a man leaves his father and his mother and cleaves to his wife and they become one flesh" (*Gn* 2:24).

Two aspects of this are important. First, *eros* is somehow rooted in man's very nature; Adam is a seeker, who "abandons his mother and father" in order to find woman; only together do the two represent complete humanity and become "one flesh". The second aspect is equally important. From the standpoint of creation, *eros* directs man towards marriage, to a bond which is unique and definitive; thus, and only thus, does it fulfil its deepest purpose. Corresponding to the image of a monotheistic God, is monogamous marriage. Marriage based on exclusive and definitive love becomes the icon of the relationship between God and his people and vice versa. God's way of loving becomes the measure of human love. This close connection between *eros* and marriage in the Bible has practically no equivalent in extra-biblical literature.

---

[8] Plato, *Symposium*, XIV-XV, 189c-192d.

19

Jesus Christ - the incarnate love of God

12. Though up to now we have been speaking mainly of the Old Testament, nevertheless the profound compenetration of the two Testaments as the one Scripture of the Christian faith has already become evident. The real novelty of the New Testament lies not so much in new ideas as in the figure of Christ himself, who gives flesh and blood to those concepts - an unprecedented realism. In the Old Testament, the novelty of the Bible did not consist merely in abstract notions but in God's unpredictable and in some sense unprecedented activity. This divine activity now takes on dramatic form when, in Jesus Christ, it is God himself who goes in search of the "stray sheep", a suffering and lost humanity. When Jesus speaks in his parables of the shepherd who goes after the lost sheep, of the woman who looks for the lost coin, of the father who goes to meet and embrace his prodigal son, these are no mere words: they constitute an explanation of his very being and activity. His death on the Cross is the culmination of that turning of God against himself in which he gives himself in order to raise man up and save him. This is love in its most radical form. By contemplating the pierced side of Christ (cf. *Jn* 19:37), we can understand the starting-point of this Encyclical Letter: "God is love" (*1 Jn* 4:8). It is there that this truth can be contemplated. It is from there that our definition of love must begin. In this contemplation the Christian discovers the path along which his life and love must move.

13. Jesus gave this act of oblation an enduring presence through his institution of the Eucharist at the Last Supper. He anticipated his death and resurrection by giving his disciples, in the bread and wine, his very self, his body and blood as the new manna (cf. *Jn* 6:31-33). The ancient world had dimly perceived that man's real food - what truly nourishes him as man - is ultimately the *Logos*, eternal wisdom: this same *Logos* now truly becomes food for us - as love. The Eucharist draws us into Jesus' act of self-oblation. More than just statically receiving the incarnate *Logos*, we enter into the very dynamic of his self-giving. The imagery of marriage between God

and Israel is now realised in a way previously inconceivable: it had meant standing in God's presence, but now it becomes union with God through sharing in Jesus' self-gift, sharing in his body and blood. The sacramental "mysticism", grounded in God's condescension towards us, operates at a radically different level and lifts us to far greater heights than anything that any human mystical elevation could ever accomplish.

14. Here we need to consider yet another aspect: this sacramental "mysticism" is social in character, for in sacramental communion I become one with the Lord, like all the other communicants. As Saint Paul says, "Because there is one bread, we who are many are one body, for we all partake of the one bread" (*1 Co* 10:17). Union with Christ is also union with all those to whom he gives himself. I cannot possess Christ just for myself; I can belong to him only in union with all those who have become, or who will become, his own. Communion draws me out of myself towards him, and thus also towards unity with all Christians. We become "one body", completely joined in a single existence. Love of God and love of neighbour are now truly united: God incarnate draws us all to himself. We can thus understand how *agape* also became a term for the Eucharist: there God's own *agape* comes to us bodily, in order to continue his work in us and through us. Only by keeping in mind this Christological and sacramental basis can we correctly understand Jesus' teaching on love. The transition which he makes from the Law and the Prophets to the twofold commandment of love of God and of neighbour, and his grounding the whole life of faith on this central precept, is not simply a matter of morality - something that could exist apart from and alongside faith in Christ and its sacramental re-actualisation. Faith, worship and *ethos* are interwoven as a single reality which takes shape in our encounter with God's *agape*. Here the usual contraposition between worship and ethics simply falls apart. "Worship" itself, Eucharistic communion, includes the reality both of being loved and of loving others in turn. A Eucharist which does not pass over into the concrete practice of love is intrinsically

fragmented. Conversely, as we shall have to consider in greater detail below, the "commandment" of love is only possible because it is more than a requirement. Love can be "commanded" because it has first been given.

15. This principle is the starting-point for understanding the great parables of Jesus. The rich man (cf. *Lk* 16:19-31) begs from his place of torment that his brothers be informed about what happens to those who simply ignore the poor man in need. Jesus takes up this cry for help as a warning to help us return to the right path. The parable of the Good Samaritan (cf. *Lk* 10:25-37) offers two particularly important clarifications. Until that time, the concept of "neighbour" was understood as referring essentially to one's countrymen and to foreigners who had settled in the land of Israel; in other words, to the closely-knit community of a single country or people. This limit is now abolished. Anyone who needs me, and whom I can help, is my neighbour. The concept of "neighbour" is now universalised, yet it remains concrete. Despite being extended to all mankind, it is not reduced to a generic, abstract and undemanding expression of love, but calls for my own practical commitment here and now. The Church has the duty to interpret ever anew this relationship between near and far with regard to the actual daily life of her members. Lastly, we should especially mention the great parable of the Last Judgement (cf. *Mt* 25:31-46), in which love becomes the criterion for the definitive decision about a human life's worth or lack thereof. Jesus identifies himself with those in need, with the hungry, the thirsty, the stranger, the naked, the sick and those in prison. "As you did it to one of the least of these my brethren, you did it to me" (*Mt* 25:40). Love of God and love of neighbour have become one: in the least of the brethren we find Jesus himself, and in Jesus we find God.

Love of God and love of neighbour

16. Having reflected on the nature of love and its meaning in biblical faith, we are left with two questions concerning our own attitude: can we love God without seeing him? And can love be

commanded? Against the double commandment of love these questions raise a double objection. No one has ever seen God, so how could we love him? Moreover, love cannot be commanded; it is ultimately a feeling that is either there or not, nor can it be produced by the will. Scripture seems to reinforce the first objection when it states: "If anyone says, 'I love God,' and hates his brother, he is a liar; for he who does not love his brother whom he has seen, cannot love God whom he has not seen" (*1 Jn* 4:20). But this text hardly excludes the love of God as something impossible. On the contrary, the whole context of the passage quoted from the *First Letter of John* shows that such love is explicitly demanded. The unbreakable bond between love of God and love of neighbour is emphasised. One is so closely connected to the other that to say that we love God becomes a lie if we are closed to our neighbour or hate him altogether. Saint John's words should rather be interpreted to mean that love of neighbour is a path that leads to the encounter with God, and that closing our eyes to our neighbour also blinds us to God.

17. True, no one has ever seen God as he is. And yet God is not totally invisible to us; he does not remain completely inaccessible. God loved us first, says the *Letter of John* quoted above (cf. 4:10), and this love of God has appeared in our midst. He has become visible in as much as he "has sent his only Son into the world, so that we might live through him" (*1 Jn* 4:9). God has made himself visible: in Jesus we are able to see the Father (cf. *Jn* 14:9). Indeed, God is visible in a number of ways. In the love-story recounted by the Bible, he comes towards us, he seeks to win our hearts, all the way to the Last Supper, to the piercing of his heart on the Cross, to his appearances after the Resurrection and to the great deeds by which, through the activity of the Apostles, he guided the nascent Church along its path. Nor has the Lord been absent from subsequent Church history: he encounters us ever anew, in the men and women who reflect his presence, in his word, in the sacraments, and especially in the Eucharist. In the Church's Liturgy, in her

prayer, in the living community of believers, we experience the love of God, we perceive his presence and we thus learn to recognise that presence in our daily lives. He has loved us first and he continues to do so; we too, then, can respond with love. God does not demand of us a feeling which we ourselves are incapable of producing. He loves us, he makes us see and experience his love, and since he has "loved us first", love can also blossom as a response within us.

In the gradual unfolding of this encounter, it is clearly revealed that love is not merely a sentiment. Sentiments come and go. A sentiment can be a marvellous first spark, but it is not the fullness of love. Earlier we spoke of the process of purification and maturation by which *eros* comes fully into its own, becomes love in the full meaning of the word. It is characteristic of mature love that it calls into play all man's potentialities; it engages the whole man, so to speak. Contact with the visible manifestations of God's love can awaken within us a feeling of joy born of the experience of being loved. But this encounter also engages our will and our intellect. Acknowledgment of the living God is one path towards love, and the "yes" of our will to his will unites our intellect, will and sentiments in the all-embracing act of love. But this process is always open-ended; love is never "finished" and complete; throughout life, it changes and matures, and thus remains faithful to itself. *Idem velle atque idem nolle*[9] - to want the same thing, and to reject the same thing - was recognised by antiquity as the authentic content of love: the one becomes similar to the other, and this leads to a community of will and thought. The love-story between God and man consists in the very fact that this communion of will increases in a communion of thought and sentiment, and thus our will and God's will increasingly coincide: God's will is no longer for me an alien will, something imposed on me from without by the commandments, but it is now my own will, based on the

---

[9] Sallust, *De coniuratione Catilinae*, XX, 4.

24

realisation that God is in fact more deeply present to me than I am to myself.[10] Then self-abandonment to God increases and God becomes our joy (cf. *Ps* 73 [72]:23-28).

18. Love of neighbour is thus shown to be possible in the way proclaimed by the Bible, by Jesus. It consists in the very fact that, in God and with God, I love even the person whom I do not like or even know. This can only take place on the basis of an intimate encounter with God, an encounter which has become a communion of will, even affecting my feelings. Then I learn to look on this other person not simply with my eyes and my feelings, but from the perspective of Jesus Christ. His friend is my friend. Going beyond exterior appearances, I perceive in others an interior desire for a sign of love, of concern. This I can offer them not only through the organisations intended for such purposes, accepting it perhaps as a political necessity. Seeing with the eyes of Christ, I can give to others much more than their outward necessities; I can give them the look of love which they crave. Here we see the necessary interplay between love of God and love of neighbour which the *First Letter of John* speaks of with such insistence. If I have no contact whatsoever with God in my life, then I cannot see in the other anything more than the other, and I am incapable of seeing in him the image of God. But if in my life I fail completely to heed others, solely out of a desire to be "devout" and to perform my "religious duties", then my relationship with God will also grow arid. It becomes merely "proper", but loveless. Only my readiness to encounter my neighbour and to show him love makes me sensitive to God as well. Only if I serve my neighbour can my eyes be opened to what God does for me and how much he loves me. The saints - consider the example of Blessed Teresa of Calcutta - constantly renewed their capacity for love of neighbour from their encounter with the Eucharistic Lord, and conversely this encounter acquired its realism and depth in their service to others. Love of

---

[10] Cf. Saint Augustine, *Confessions*, III, 6, 11: CCL 27, 32.

25

God and love of neighbour are thus inseparable, they form a single commandment. But both live from the love of God who has loved us first. No longer is it a question, then, of a "commandment" imposed from without and calling for the impossible, but rather of a freely-bestowed experience of love from within, a love which by its very nature must then be shared with others. Love grows through love. Love is "divine" because it comes from God and unites us to God; through this unifying process it makes us a "we" which transcends our divisions and makes us one, until in the end God is "all in all" (*1 Co* 15:28).

PART II

CARITAS

THE PRACTICE OF LOVE BY THE CHURCH AS A "COMMUNITY OF LOVE"

The Church's charitable activity as a manifestation of Trinitarian love

19. "If you see charity, you see the Trinity", wrote Saint Augustine.[11] In the foregoing reflections, we have been able to focus our attention on the Pierced one (cf. *Jn* 19:37; *Zc* 12:10), recognising the plan of the Father who, moved by love (cf. *Jn* 3:16), sent his only-begotten Son into the world to redeem man. By dying on the Cross - as Saint John tells us - Jesus "gave up his Spirit" (*Jn* 19:30), anticipating the gift of the Holy Spirit that he would make after his Resurrection (cf. *Jn* 20:22). This was to fulfil the promise of "rivers of living water" that would flow out of the hearts of believers, through the outpouring of the Spirit (cf. *Jn* 7:38-39). The Spirit, in fact, is that interior power which harmonises their hearts with Christ's heart and moves them to love their brethren as Christ loved them, when he bent down to wash the feet of the disciples (cf. *Jn* 13:1-13) and above all when he gave his life for us (cf. *Jn* 13:1; 15:13).

The Spirit is also the energy which transforms the heart of the ecclesial community, so that it becomes a witness before the world to the love of the Father, who wishes to make humanity a single family in his Son. The entire activity of the Church is an expression of a love that seeks the integral good of man: it seeks his evangelisation through Word and Sacrament, an undertaking that is often heroic in the way it is acted out in history; and it seeks to

---

[11] *De Trinitate*, VIII, 8, 12: CCL 50, 287.

27

promote man in the various arenas of life and human activity. Love is therefore the service that the Church carries out in order to attend constantly to man's sufferings and his needs, including material needs. And this is the aspect, this *service of charity*, on which I want to focus in the second part of the Encyclical.

Charity as a responsibility of the Church

20. Love of neighbour, grounded in the love of God, is first and foremost a responsibility for each individual member of the faithful, but it is also a responsibility for the entire ecclesial community at every level: from the local community to the particular Church and to the Church universal in its entirety. As a community, the Church must practise love. Love thus needs to be organised if it is to be an ordered service to the community. The awareness of this responsibility has had a constitutive relevance in the Church from the beginning: "All who believed were together and had all things in common; and they sold their possessions and goods and distributed them to all, as any had need" (*Ac* 2:44-5). In these words, Saint Luke provides a kind of definition of the Church, whose constitutive elements include fidelity to the "teaching of the Apostles", "communion" (*koinonia*), "the breaking of the bread" and "prayer" (cf. *Ac* 2:42). The element of "communion" (*koinonia*) is not initially defined, but appears concretely in the verses quoted above: it consists in the fact that believers hold all things in common and that among them, there is no longer any distinction between rich and poor (cf. also *Ac* 4:32-37). As the Church grew, this radical form of material communion could not in fact be preserved. But its essential core remained: within the community of believers there can never be room for a poverty that denies anyone what is needed for a dignified life.

21. A decisive step in the difficult search for ways of putting this fundamental ecclesial principle into practice is illustrated in the choice of the seven, which marked the origin of the diaconal office (cf. *Ac* 6:5-6). In the early Church, in fact, with regard to the daily

distribution to widows, a disparity had arisen between Hebrew speakers and Greek speakers. The Apostles, who had been entrusted primarily with "prayer" (the Eucharist and the liturgy) and the "ministry of the word", felt over-burdened by "serving tables", so they decided to reserve to themselves the principal duty and to designate for the other task, also necessary in the Church, a group of seven persons. Nor was this group to carry out a purely mechanical work of distribution: they were to be men "full of the Spirit and of wisdom" (cf. *Ac* 6:1-6). In other words, the social service which they were meant to provide was absolutely concrete, yet at the same time it was also a spiritual service; theirs was a truly spiritual office which carried out an essential responsibility of the Church, namely a well-ordered love of neighbour. With the formation of this group of seven, "*diaconia*" - the ministry of charity exercised in a communitarian, orderly way - became part of the fundamental structure of the Church.

22. As the years went by and the Church spread further afield, the exercise of charity became established as one of her essential activities, along with the administration of the sacraments and the proclamation of the word: love for widows and orphans, prisoners, and the sick and needy of every kind, is as essential to her as the ministry of the sacraments and preaching of the Gospel. The Church cannot neglect the service of charity any more than she can neglect the Sacraments and the Word. A few references will suffice to demonstrate this. Justin Martyr († c.155) in speaking of the Christians' celebration of Sunday, also mentions their charitable activity, linked with the Eucharist as such. Those who are able make offerings in accordance with their means, each as he or she wishes; the Bishop in turn makes use of these to support orphans, widows, the sick and those who for other reasons find themselves in need, such as prisoners and foreigners.[12] The great Christian writer Tertullian († after 220) relates how the pagans were struck by the

---

[12] Cf. *I Apologia*, 67: PG 6, 429.

Christians' concern for the needy of every sort.[13] And when Ignatius of Antioch († c.117) described the Church of Rome as "presiding in charity (*agape*)",[14] we may assume that with this definition he also intended in some sense to express her concrete charitable activity.

23. Here it might be helpful to allude to the earliest legal structures associated with the service of charity in the Church. Towards the middle of the fourth century we see the development in Egypt of the "*diaconia*": the institution within each monastery responsible for all works of relief, that is to say, for the service of charity. By the sixth century this institution had evolved into a corporation with full juridical standing, which the civil authorities themselves entrusted with part of the grain for public distribution. In Egypt not only each monastery, but each individual Diocese eventually had its own *diaconia*; this institution then developed in both East and West. Pope Gregory the Great († 604) mentions the *diaconia* of Naples, while in Rome the *diaconiae* are documented from the seventh and eighth centuries. But charitable activity on behalf of the poor and suffering was naturally an essential part of the Church of Rome from the very beginning, based on the principles of Christian life given in the Acts of the Apostles. It found a vivid expression in the case of the deacon Lawrence († 258). The dramatic description of Lawrence's martyrdom was known to Saint Ambrose († 397) and it provides a fundamentally authentic picture of the saint. As the one responsible for the care of the poor in Rome, Lawrence had been given a period of time, after the capture of the Pope and of Lawrence's fellow deacons, to collect the treasures of the Church and hand them over to the civil authorities. He distributed to the poor whatever funds were available and then presented to the authorities the poor themselves as the real treasure of the Church.[15] Whatever historical reliability one attributes to these details,

---

[13] Cf. *Apologeticum*, 39, 7: PL 1, 468.

[14] *Ep. ad Rom., Inscr:* PG 5, 801.

[15] Cf. Saint Ambrose, *De officiis ministrorum*, II, 28, 140: PL 16, 141.

Lawrence has always remained present in the Church's memory as a great exponent of ecclesial charity.

24. A mention of the emperor Julian the Apostate (†363) can also show how essential the early Church considered the organised practice of charity. As a child of six years, Julian witnessed the assassination of his father, brother and other family members by the guards of the imperial palace; rightly or wrongly, he blamed this brutal act on the Emperor Constantius, who passed himself off as an outstanding Christian. The Christian faith was thus definitively discredited in his eyes. Upon becoming emperor, Julian decided to restore paganism, the ancient Roman religion, while reforming it in the hope of making it the driving force behind the empire. In this project he was amply inspired by Christianity. He established a hierarchy of metropolitans and priests who were to foster love of God and neighbour. In one of his letters,[16] he wrote that the sole aspect of Christianity which had impressed him was the Church's charitable activity. He thus considered it essential for his new pagan religion that, alongside the system of the Church's charity, an equivalent activity of its own be established. According to him, this was the reason for the popularity of the "Galileans". They needed now to be imitated and outdone. In this way, then, the Emperor confirmed that charity was a decisive feature of the Christian community, the Church.

25. Thus far, two essential facts have emerged from our reflections:

(a) The Church's deepest nature is expressed in her three-fold responsibility: of proclaiming the word of God (*kerygma-martyria*), celebrating the sacraments (*leitourgia*), and exercising the ministry of charity (*diakonia*). These duties presuppose each other and are inseparable. For the Church, charity is not a kind of welfare activity which could equally well be left to others, but is a part of her nature, an indispensable expression of her very being.[17]

---

[16] Cf. *Ep.* 83: J. Bidez, *L'Empereur Julien. Œuvres complètes*, Paris 19602, v. I, 2a, p. 145.

[17] Cf. Congregation for Bishops, Directory for the Pastoral Ministry of Bishops *Apostolorum Successores* (22nd February 2004), 194, Vatican City 2004, p. 213.

(b) The Church is God's family in the world. In this family no one ought to go without the necessities of life. Yet at the same time *caritas-agape* extends beyond the frontiers of the Church. The parable of the Good Samaritan remains as a standard which imposes universal love towards the needy whom we encounter "by chance" (cf. *Lk* 10:31), whoever they may be. Without in any way detracting from this commandment of universal love, the Church also has a specific responsibility: within the ecclesial family no member should suffer through being in need. The teaching of the *Letter to the Galatians* is emphatic: "So then, as we have opportunity, let us do good to all, and especially to those who are of the household of faith" (6:10).

Justice and Charity

26. Since the nineteenth century, an objection has been raised to the Church's charitable activity, subsequently developed with particular insistence by Marxism: the poor, it is claimed, do not need charity but justice. Works of charity - almsgiving - are in effect a way for the rich to shirk their obligation to work for justice and a means of soothing their consciences, while preserving their own status and robbing the poor of their rights. Instead of contributing through individual works of charity to maintaining the *status quo*, we need to build a just social order in which all receive their share of the world's goods and no longer have to depend on charity. There is admittedly some truth to this argument, but also much that is mistaken. It is true that the pursuit of justice must be a fundamental norm of the State and that the aim of a just social order is to guarantee to each person, according to the principle of subsidiarity, his share of the community's goods. This has always been emphasised by Christian teaching on the State and by the Church's social doctrine. Historically, the issue of the just ordering of the collectivity had taken a new dimension with the industrialisation of society in the nineteenth century. The rise of modern industry caused the old social structures to collapse, while the growth of a class of salaried workers provoked radical changes in the fabric of

society. The relationship between capital and labour now became the decisive issue - an issue which in that form was previously unknown. Capital and the means of production were now the new source of power which, concentrated in the hands of a few, led to the suppression of the rights of the working classes, against which they had to rebel.

27. It must be admitted that the Church's leadership was slow to realise that the issue of the just structuring of society needed to be approached in a new way. There were some pioneers, such as Bishop Ketteler of Mainz (†1877), and concrete needs were met by a growing number of groups, associations, leagues, federations and, in particular, by the new religious orders founded in the nineteenth century to combat poverty, disease and the need for better education. In 1891, the papal magisterium intervened with the Encyclical *Rerum Novarum* of Leo XIII. This was followed in 1931 by Pius XI's Encyclical *Quadragesimo Anno*. In 1961 Blessed John XXIII published the Encyclical *Mater et Magistra*, while Paul VI, in the Encyclical *Populorum Progressio* (1967) and in the Apostolic Letter *Octogesima Adveniens* (1971), insistently addressed the social problem, which had meanwhile become especially acute in Latin America. My great predecessor John Paul II left us a trilogy of social Encyclicals: *Laborem Exercens* (1981), *Sollicitudo Rei Socialis* (1987) and finally *Centesimus Annus* (1991). Faced with new situations and issues, Catholic social teaching thus gradually developed, and has now found a comprehensive presentation in the *Compendium of the Social Doctrine of the Church* published in 2004 by the Pontifical Council *Iustitia et Pax*. Marxism had seen world revolution and its preliminaries as the panacea for the social problem: revolution and the subsequent collectivisation of the means of production, so it was claimed, would immediately change things for the better. This illusion has vanished. In today's complex situation, not least because of the growth of a globalised economy, the Church's social doctrine has become a set of fundamental guidelines offering approaches that are valid even beyond the confines of the Church: in

33

the face of ongoing development these guidelines need to be addressed in the context of dialogue with all those seriously concerned for humanity and for the world in which we live.

28. In order to define more accurately the relationship between the necessary commitment to justice and the ministry of charity, two fundamental situations need to be considered:

(a) The just ordering of society and the State is a central responsibility of politics. As Augustine once said, a State which is not governed according to justice would be just a bunch of thieves: *"Remota itaque iustitia quid sunt regna nisi magna latrocinia?"*[18] Fundamental to Christianity is the distinction between what belongs to Caesar and what belongs to God (cf. *Mt* 22:21), in other words, the distinction between Church and State, or, as the Second Vatican Council puts it, the autonomy of the temporal sphere.[19] The State may not impose religion, yet it must guarantee religious freedom and harmony between the followers of different religions. For her part, the Church, as the social expression of Christian faith, has a proper independence and is structured on the basis of her faith as a community which the State must recognise. The two spheres are distinct, yet always interrelated.

Justice is both the aim and the intrinsic criterion of all politics. Politics is more than a mere mechanism for defining the rules of public life: its origin and its goal are found in justice, which by its very nature has to do with ethics. The State must inevitably face the question of how justice can be achieved here and now. But this presupposes an even more radical question: what is justice? The problem is one of practical reason; but if reason is to be exercised properly, it must undergo constant purification, since it can never be completely free of the danger of a certain ethical blindness caused by the dazzling effect of power and special interests.

---

[18] *De Civitate Dei*, IV, 4: CCL 47, 102.

[19] Cf. Pastoral Constitution on the Church in the Modern World *Gaudium et Spes*, 36.

Here politics and faith meet. Faith by its specific nature is an encounter with the living God - an encounter opening up new horizons extending beyond the sphere of reason. But it is also a purifying force for reason itself. From God's standpoint, faith liberates reason from its blind spots and therefore helps it to be ever more fully itself. Faith enables reason to do its work more effectively and to see its proper object more clearly. This is where Catholic social doctrine has its place: it has no intention of giving the Church power over the State. Even less is it an attempt to impose on those who do not share the faith ways of thinking and modes of conduct proper to faith. Its aim is simply to help purify reason and to contribute, here and now, to the acknowledgment and attainment of what is just.

The Church's social teaching argues on the basis of reason and natural law, namely, on the basis of what is in accord with the nature of every human being. It recognises that it is not the Church's responsibility to make this teaching prevail in political life. Rather, the Church wishes to help form consciences in political life and to stimulate greater insight into the authentic requirements of justice as well as greater readiness to act accordingly, even when this might involve conflict with situations of personal interest. Building a just social and civil order, wherein each person receives what is his or her due, is an essential task which every generation must take up anew. As a political task, this cannot be the Church's immediate responsibility. Yet, since it is also a most important human responsibility, the Church is duty-bound to offer, through the purification of reason and through ethical formation, her own specific contribution towards understanding the requirements of justice and achieving them politically.

The Church cannot and must not take upon herself the political battle to bring about the most just society possible. She cannot and must not replace the State. Yet at the same time she cannot and must not remain on the sidelines in the fight for justice. She has to play her part through rational argument and she has to reawaken the spiritual energy without which justice, which always demands sacrifice, cannot prevail and prosper. A just society must be the achievement of politics, not of the Church. Yet the promotion of justice through efforts to bring about openness of mind and will to the demands of the common good is something which concerns the Church deeply.

(b) Love - *caritas* - will always prove necessary, even in the most just society. There is no ordering of the State so just that it can eliminate the need for a service of love. Whoever wants to eliminate love is preparing to eliminate man as such. There will always be suffering which cries out for consolation and help. There will always be loneliness. There will always be situations of material need where help in the form of concrete love of neighbour is indispensable.[20] The State which would provide everything, absorbing everything into itself, would ultimately become a mere bureaucracy incapable of guaranteeing the very thing which the suffering person - every person - needs: namely, loving personal concern. We do not need a State which regulates and controls everything, but a State which, in accordance with the principle of subsidiarity, generously acknowledges and supports initiatives arising from the different social forces and combines spontaneity with closeness to those in need. The Church is one of those living forces: she is alive with the love enkindled by the Spirit of Christ. This love does not simply offer people material help, but refreshment and care for their souls, something which often is even more necessary than material support. In the end, the claim that just social structures would make works of charity superfluous masks a materialist conception of man: the mistaken notion that man can live "by bread alone" (*Mt* 4:4; cf. *Dt* 8:3) - a conviction that demeans man and ultimately disregards all that is specifically human.

29. We can now determine more precisely, in the life of the Church, the relationship between commitment to the just ordering of the State and society on the one hand, and organised charitable activity

---

[20] Cf. Congregation for Bishops, Directory for the Pastoral Ministry of Bishops *Apostolorum Successores* (22nd February 2004), 197, Vatican City 2004, p. 217.

on the other. We have seen that the formation of just structures is not directly the duty of the Church, but belongs to the world of politics, the sphere of the autonomous use of reason. The Church has an indirect duty here, in that she is called to contribute to the purification of reason and to the reawakening of those moral forces without which just structures are neither established nor prove effective in the long run.

The direct duty to work for a just ordering of society, on the other hand, is proper to the lay faithful. As citizens of the State, they are called to take part in public life in a personal capacity. So they cannot relinquish their participation "in the many different economic, social, legislative, administrative and cultural areas, which are intended to promote organically and institutionally the common good."[21] The mission of the lay faithful is therefore to configure social life correctly, respecting its legitimate autonomy and cooperating with other citizens according to their respective competences and fulfilling their own responsibility.[22] Even if the specific expressions of ecclesial charity can never be confused with the activity of the State, it still remains true that charity must animate the entire lives of the lay faithful and therefore also their political activity, lived as "social charity".[23]

The Church's charitable organisations, on the other hand, constitute an *opus proprium*, a task agreeable to her, in which she does not cooperate collaterally, but acts as a subject with direct responsibility, doing what corresponds to her nature. The Church can never be exempted from practising charity as an organised activity of believers, and on the other hand, there will never be a situation where the charity of each individual Christian is unnecessary, because in addition to justice man needs, and will always need, love.

---

[21] John Paul II, Post-Synodal Apostolic Exhortation *Christifideles Laici* (30th December 1988), 42: AAS 81 (1989), 472.

[22] Cf. Congregation for the Doctrine of the Faith, *Doctrinal Note on Some Questions Regarding the Participation of Catholics in Political Life* (24th November 2002), 1: *L'Osservatore Romano*, English edition, 22nd January 2003, p. 5.

[23] *Catechism of the Catholic Church*, 1939.

The multiple structures of charitable service in the social context of the present day

30. Before attempting to define the specific profile of the Church's activities in the service of man, I now wish to consider the overall situation of the struggle for justice and love in the world of today.

(a) Today the means of mass communication have made our planet smaller, rapidly narrowing the distance between different peoples and cultures. This "togetherness" at times gives rise to misunderstandings and tensions, yet our ability to know almost instantly about the needs of others challenges us to share their situation and their difficulties. Despite the great advances made in science and technology, each day we see how much suffering there is in the world on account of different kinds of poverty, both material and spiritual. Our times call for a new readiness to assist our neighbours in need. The Second Vatican Council had made this point very clearly: "Now that, through better means of communication, distances between peoples have been almost eliminated, charitable activity can and should embrace all people and all needs."[24]

On the other hand - and here we see one of the challenging yet also positive sides of the process of globalisation - we now have at our disposal numerous means for offering humanitarian assistance to our brothers and sisters in need, not least modern systems of distributing food and clothing, and of providing housing and care. Concern for our neighbour transcends the confines of national communities and has increasingly broadened its horizon to the whole world. The Second Vatican Council rightly observed that "among the signs of our times, one particularly worthy of note is a growing, inescapable sense of solidarity between all peoples."[25] State agencies and humanitarian associations work to promote this, the former mainly through subsidies or tax relief, the latter by

---

[24] Decree on the Apostolate of the Laity *Apostolicam Actuositatem*, 8.

[25] Ibid., 14.

making available considerable resources. The solidarity shown by civil society thus significantly surpasses that shown by individuals.

(b) This situation has led to the birth and the growth of many forms of cooperation between State and Church agencies, which have borne fruit. Church agencies, with their transparent operation and their faithfulness to the duty of witnessing to love, are able to give a Christian quality to the civil agencies too, favouring a mutual coordination that can only redound to the effectiveness of charitable service.[26] Numerous organisations for charitable or philanthropic purposes have also been established and these are committed to achieving adequate humanitarian solutions to the social and political problems of the day. Significantly, our time has also seen the growth and spread of different kinds of volunteer work, which assume responsibility for providing a variety of services.[27] I wish here to offer a special word of gratitude and appreciation to all those who take part in these activities in whatever way. For young people, this widespread involvement constitutes a school of life which offers them a formation in solidarity and in readiness to offer others not simply material aid but their very selves. The anti-culture of death, which finds expression for example in drug use, is thus countered by an unselfish love which shows itself to be a culture of life by the very willingness to "lose itself" (cf. *Lk* 17:33 *et passim*) for others.

In the Catholic Church, and also in the other Churches and Ecclesial Communities, new forms of charitable activity have arisen, while other, older ones have taken on new life and energy. In these new forms, it is often possible to establish a fruitful link between evangelisation and works of charity. Here I would clearly reaffirm what my great predecessor John Paul II wrote in his

---

[26] Cf. Congregation for Bishops, Directory for the Pastoral Ministry of Bishops *Apostolorum Successores* (22nd February 2004), 195, Vatican City 2004, pp. 214-216.

[27] Cf. John Paul II, Post-Synodal Apostolic Exhortation *Christifideles Laici* (30th December 1988), 41: AAS 81 (1989), 470-472.

Encyclical *Sollicitudo Rei Socialis*[28] when he asserted the readiness of the Catholic Church to cooperate with the charitable agencies of these Churches and Communities, since we all have the same fundamental motivation and look towards the same goal: a true humanism, which acknowledges that man is made in the image of God and wants to help him to live in a way consonant with that dignity. His Encyclical *Ut Unum Sint* emphasised that the building of a better world requires Christians to speak with a united voice in working to inculcate "respect for the rights and needs of everyone, especially the poor, the lowly and the defenceless."[29] Here I would like to express my satisfaction that this appeal has found a wide resonance in numerous initiatives throughout the world.

The distinctiveness of the Church's charitable activity

31. The increase in diversified organisations engaged in meeting various human needs is ultimately due to the fact that the command of love of neighbour is inscribed by the Creator in man's very nature. It is also a result of the presence of Christianity in the world, since Christianity constantly revives and acts out this imperative, so often profoundly obscured in the course of time. The reform of paganism attempted by the emperor Julian the Apostate is only an initial example of this effect; here we see how the power of Christianity spread well beyond the frontiers of the Christian faith. For this reason, it is very important that the Church's charitable activity maintains all of its splendour and does not become just another form of social assistance. So what are the essential elements of Christian and ecclesial charity?

(a) Following the example given in the parable of the Good Samaritan, Christian charity is first of all the simple response to immediate needs and specific situations: feeding the hungry, clothing the naked, caring for and healing the sick, visiting those in

---

[28] Cf. No. 32: AAS 80 (1988), 556.

[29] No. 43: AAS 87 (1995), 946.

prison, etc. The Church's charitable organisations, beginning with those of *Caritas* (at diocesan, national and international levels), ought to do everything in their power to provide the resources and above all the personnel needed for this work. Individuals who care for those in need must first be professionally competent: they should be properly trained in what to do and how to do it, and committed to continuing care. Yet, while professional competence is a primary, fundamental requirement, it is not of itself sufficient. We are dealing with human beings, and human beings always need something more than technically proper care. They need humanity. They need heartfelt concern. Those who work for the Church's charitable organisations must be distinguished by the fact that they do not merely meet the needs of the moment, but they dedicate themselves to others with heartfelt concern, enabling them to experience the richness of their humanity. Consequently, in addition to their necessary professional training, these charity workers need a "formation of the heart": they need to be led to that encounter with God in Christ which awakens their love and opens their spirits to others. As a result, love of neighbour will no longer be for them a commandment imposed, so to speak, from without, but a consequence deriving from their faith, a faith which becomes active through love (cf. *Ga* 5:6).

(b) Christian charitable activity must be independent of parties and ideologies. It is not a means of changing the world ideologically, and it is not at the service of worldly stratagems, but it is a way of making present here and now the love which man always needs. The modern age, particularly from the nineteenth century on, has been dominated by various versions of a philosophy of progress whose most radical form is Marxism. Part of Marxist strategy is the theory of impoverishment: in a situation of unjust power, it is claimed, anyone who engages in charitable initiatives is actually serving that unjust system, making it appear at least to some extent tolerable. This in turn slows down a potential revolution and thus blocks the struggle for a better world. Seen in this way, charity is rejected and attacked as a means of preserving the *status quo*. What we have here, though, is really an inhuman philosophy. People of the present are sacrificed to the *moloch* of the future - a future whose effective realisation is at best doubtful. One does not make the world more human by refusing to act humanely here and now. We contribute to a better world only by personally doing good now, with full commitment and wherever we have the opportunity, independently of partisan strategies and programmes. The Christian's programme - the programme of the Good Samaritan, the programme of Jesus - is "a heart which sees". This heart sees where love is needed and acts accordingly. Obviously when charitable activity is carried out by the Church as a communitarian initiative, the spontaneity of individuals must be combined with planning, foresight and cooperation with other similar institutions.

(c) Charity, furthermore, cannot be used as a means of engaging in what is nowadays considered proselytism. Love is free; it is not practised as a way of achieving other ends.[30] But this does not mean that charitable activity must somehow leave God and Christ aside. For it is always concerned with the whole man. Often the deepest cause of suffering is the very absence of God. Those who practise charity in the Church's name will never seek to impose the Church's faith upon others. They realise that a pure and generous love is the best witness to the God in whom we believe and by whom we are driven to love. A Christian knows when it is time to speak of God and when it is better to say nothing and to let love alone speak. He knows that God is love (cf. *1 Jn* 4:8) and that God's presence is felt at the very time when the only thing we do is to love. He knows - to return to the questions raised earlier - that disdain for love is disdain for God and man alike; it is an attempt to do without God. Consequently, the best defence of God and man consists precisely in love. It is the responsibility of the Church's

---

[30] Cf. Congregation for Bishops, Directory for the Pastoral Ministry of Bishops *Apostolorum Successores* (22nd February 2004), 196, Vatican City 2004, p. 216.

charitable organisations to reinforce this awareness in their members, so that by their activity - as well as their words, their silence, their example - they may be credible witnesses to Christ.

Those responsible for the Church's charitable activity

32. Finally, we must turn our attention once again to those who are responsible for carrying out the Church's charitable activity. As our preceding reflections have made clear, the true subject of the various Catholic organisations that carry out a ministry of charity is the Church herself - at all levels, from the parishes, through the particular Churches, to the universal Church. For this reason it was most opportune that my venerable predecessor Paul VI established the Pontifical Council *Cor Unum* as the agency of the Holy See responsible for orienting and coordinating the organisations and charitable activities promoted by the Catholic Church. In conformity with the episcopal structure of the Church, the Bishops, as successors of the Apostles, are charged with primary responsibility for carrying out in the particular Churches the programme set forth in the *Acts of the Apostles* (cf. 2:42-44): today as in the past, the Church as God's family must be a place where help is given and received, and at the same time, a place where people are also prepared to serve those outside her confines who are in need of help. In the rite of episcopal ordination, prior to the act of consecration itself, the candidate must respond to several questions which express the essential elements of his office and recall the duties of his future ministry. He promises expressly to be, in the Lord's name, welcoming and merciful to the poor and to all those in need of consolation and assistance.[31] The *Code of Canon Law*, in the canons on the ministry of the Bishop, does not expressly mention charity as a specific sector of episcopal activity, but speaks in general terms of the Bishop's responsibility for coordinating the different works of the apostolate with due regard for their proper

---

[31] Cf. Pontificale Romanum, *De ordinatione episcopi*, 43.

43

character.[32] Recently, however, the *Directory for the Pastoral Ministry of Bishops* explored more specifically the duty of charity as a responsibility incumbent upon the whole Church and upon each Bishop in his Diocese,[33] and it emphasised that the exercise of charity is an action of the Church as such, and that, like the ministry of Word and Sacrament, it too has been an essential part of her mission from the very beginning.[34]

33. With regard to the personnel who carry out the Church's charitable activity on the practical level, the essential has already been said: they must not be inspired by ideologies aimed at improving the world, but should rather be guided by the faith which works through love (cf. *Ga* 5:6). Consequently, more than anything, they must be persons moved by Christ's love, persons whose hearts Christ has conquered with his love, awakening within them a love of neighbour. The criterion inspiring their activity should be Saint Paul's statement in the *Second Letter to the Corinthians*: "the love of Christ urges us on" (5:14). The consciousness that, in Christ, God has given himself for us, even unto death, must inspire us to live no longer for ourselves but for him, and, with him, for others. Whoever loves Christ loves the Church, and desires the Church to be increasingly the image and instrument of the love which flows from Christ. The personnel of every Catholic charitable organisation want to work with the Church and therefore with the Bishop, so that the love of God can spread throughout the world. By their sharing in the Church's practice of love, they wish to be witnesses of God and of Christ, and they wish for this very reason freely to do good to all.

34. Interior openness to the Catholic dimension of the Church cannot fail to dispose charity workers to work in harmony with other organisations in serving various forms of need, but in a way

---

[32] Cf. can. 394; *Code of Canons of the Eastern Churches*, can. 203.

[33] Cf. Nos. 193-198: pp. 212-219.

[34] Ibid., 194: pp. 213-214.

that respects what is distinctive about the service which Christ requested of his disciples. Saint Paul, in his hymn to charity (cf. *1 Co* 13), teaches us that it is always more than activity alone: "If I give away all I have, and if I deliver my body to be burned, but do not have love, I gain nothing" (v. 3). This hymn must be the *Magna Carta* of all ecclesial service; it sums up all the reflections on love which I have offered throughout this Encyclical Letter. Practical activity will always be insufficient, unless it visibly expresses a love for man, a love nourished by an encounter with Christ. My deep personal sharing in the needs and sufferings of others becomes a sharing of my very self with them: if my gift is not to prove a source of humiliation, I must give to others not only something that is my own, but my very self; I must be personally present in my gift.

35. This proper way of serving others also leads to humility. The one who serves does not consider himself superior to the one served, however miserable his situation at the moment may be. Christ took the lowest place in the world - the Cross - and by this radical humility he redeemed us and constantly comes to our aid. Those who are in a position to help others will realise that in doing so they themselves receive help; being able to help others is no merit or achievement of their own. This duty is a grace. The more we do for others, the more we understand and can appropriate the words of Christ: "We are useless servants" (*Lk* 17:10). We recognise that we are not acting on the basis of any superiority or greater personal efficiency, but because the Lord has graciously enabled us to do so. There are times when the burden of need and our own limitations might tempt us to become discouraged. But precisely then we are helped by the knowledge that, in the end, we are only instruments in the Lord's hands; and this knowledge frees us from the presumption of thinking that we alone are personally responsible for building a better world. In all humility we will do what we can, and in all humility we will entrust the rest to the Lord. It is God who governs the world, not we. We offer him our service only to the extent that we can, and for as long as he grants us the

strength. To do all we can with what strength we have, however, is the task which keeps the good servant of Jesus Christ always at work: "The love of Christ urges us on" (2 *Co* 5:14).

36. When we consider the immensity of others' needs, we can, on the one hand, be driven towards an ideology that would aim at doing what God's governance of the world apparently cannot: fully resolving every problem. Or we can be tempted to give in to inertia, since it would seem that in any event nothing can be accomplished. At such times, a living relationship with Christ is decisive if we are to keep on the right path, without falling into an arrogant contempt for man, something not only unconstructive but actually destructive, or surrendering to a resignation which would prevent us from being guided by love in the service of others. Prayer, as a means of drawing ever new strength from Christ, is concretely and urgently needed. People who pray are not wasting their time, even though the situation appears desperate and seems to call for action alone. Piety does not undermine the struggle against the poverty of our neighbours, however extreme. In the example of Blessed Teresa of Calcutta we have a clear illustration of the fact that time devoted to God in prayer not only does not detract from effective and loving service to our neighbour but is in fact the inexhaustible source of that service. In her letter for Lent 1996, Blessed Teresa wrote to her lay co-workers: "We need this deep connection with God in our daily life. How can we obtain it? By prayer".

37. It is time to reaffirm the importance of prayer in the face of the activism and the growing secularism of many Christians engaged in charitable work. Clearly, the Christian who prays does not claim to be able to change God's plans or correct what he has foreseen. Rather, he seeks an encounter with the Father of Jesus Christ, asking God to be present with the consolation of the Spirit to him and his work. A personal relationship with God and an abandonment to his will can prevent man from being demeaned and save him from falling prey to the teaching of fanaticism and

terrorism. An authentically religious attitude prevents man from presuming to judge God, accusing him of allowing poverty and failing to have compassion for his creatures. When people claim to build a case against God in defence of man, on whom can they depend when human activity proves powerless?

38. Certainly Job could complain before God about the presence of incomprehensible and apparently unjustified suffering in the world. In his pain he cried out: "Oh, that I knew where I might find him, that I might come even to his seat!...I would learn what he would answer me, and understand what he would say to me. Would he contend with me in the greatness of his power? ... Therefore I am terrified at his presence; when I consider, I am in dread of him. God has made my heart faint; the Almighty has terrified me" (23:3, 5-6, 15-16). Often we cannot understand why God refrains from intervening. Yet he does not prevent us from crying out, like Jesus on the Cross: "My God, my God, why have you forsaken me?" (*Mt* 27:46) We should continue asking this question in prayerful dialogue before his face: "Lord, holy and true, how long will it be?" (*Rv* 6:10) It is Saint Augustine who gives us faith's answer to our sufferings: "*Si comprehendis, non est Deus*" - "if you understand him, he is not God."[35] Our protest is not meant to challenge God, or to suggest that error, weakness or indifference can be found in him. For the believer, it is impossible to imagine that God is powerless or that "perhaps he is asleep" (cf. *1 K* 18:27). Instead, our crying out is, as it was for Jesus on the Cross, the deepest and most radical way of affirming our faith in his sovereign power. Even in their bewilderment and failure to understand the world around them, Christians continue to believe in the "goodness and loving kindness of God" (*Ti* 3:4). Immersed like everyone else in the dramatic complexity of historical events, they remain unshakably certain that God is our Father and loves us, even when his silence remains incomprehensible.

---

[35] *Sermo* 52, 16: PL 38, 360.

39. Faith, hope and charity go together. Hope is practised through the virtue of patience, which continues to do good even in the face of apparent failure, and through the virtue of humility, which accepts God's mystery and trusts him even at times of darkness. Faith tells us that God has given his Son for our sakes and gives us the victorious certainty that it is really true: God is love! It thus transforms our impatience and our doubts into the sure hope that God holds the world in his hands and that, as the dramatic imagery of the end of the *Book of Revelation* points out, in spite of all darkness he ultimately triumphs in glory. Faith, which sees the love of God revealed in the pierced heart of Jesus on the Cross, gives rise to love. Love is the light - and in the end, the only light - that can always illuminate a world grown dim and give us the courage needed to keep living and working. Love is possible, and we are able to practise it because we are created in the image of God. To experience love and in this way to cause the light of God to enter into the world - this is the invitation I would like to extend with the present Encyclical.

CONCLUSION

40. Finally, let us consider the saints, who exercised charity in an exemplary way. Our thoughts turn especially to Martin of Tours (†397), the soldier who became a monk and a bishop: he is almost like an icon, illustrating the irreplaceable value of the individual testimony to charity. At the gates of Amiens, Martin gave half of his cloak to a poor man: Jesus himself, that night, appeared to him in a dream wearing that cloak, confirming the permanent validity of the Gospel saying: "I was naked and you clothed me...as you did it to one of the least of these my brethren, you did it to me" (*Mt* 25:36, 40).[36] Yet in the history of the Church, how many other testimonies to charity could be quoted! In particular, the entire monastic movement, from its origins with Saint Anthony the Abbot (†356), expresses an immense service of charity towards neighbour. In his encounter "face to face" with the God who is Love, the monk senses the impelling need to transform his whole life into service of neighbour, in addition to service of God. This explains the great emphasis on hospitality, refuge and care of the infirm in the vicinity of the monasteries. It also explains the immense initiatives of human welfare and Christian formation, aimed above all at the very poor, who became the object of care firstly for the monastic and mendicant orders, and later for the various male and female religious institutes all through the history of the Church. The figures of saints such as Francis of Assisi, Ignatius of Loyola, John of God, Camillus of Lellis, Vincent de Paul, Louise de Marillac, Giuseppe B. Cottolengo, John Bosco, Luigi Orione, Teresa of Calcutta to name but a few - stand out as lasting models of social charity for all people of good will. The saints are the true bearers of light within history, for they are men and women of faith, hope and love.

41. Outstanding among the saints is Mary, Mother of the Lord and mirror of all holiness. In the *Gospel of Luke* we find her engaged in a service of charity to her cousin Elizabeth, with whom she remained

---

[36] Cf. Sulpicius Severus, *Vita Sancti Martini*, 3, 1-3: SCh 133, 256-258.

for "about three months" (1:56) so as to assist her in the final phase of her pregnancy. *"Magnificat anima mea Dominum"*, she says on the occasion of that visit, "My soul magnifies the Lord" (*Lk* 1:46). In these words she expresses her whole programme of life: not setting herself at the centre, but leaving space for God, who is encountered both in prayer and in service of neighbour - only then does goodness enter the world. Mary's greatness consists in the fact that she wants to magnify God, not herself. She is lowly: her only desire is to be the handmaid of the Lord (cf. *Lk* 1:38, 48). She knows that she will only contribute to the salvation of the world if, rather than carrying out her own projects, she places herself completely at the disposal of God's initiatives. Mary is a woman of hope: only because she believes in God's promises and awaits the salvation of Israel, can the angel visit her and call her to the decisive service of these promises. Mary is a woman of faith: "Blessed are you who believed", Elizabeth says to her (cf. *Lk* 1:45). The *Magnificat* - a portrait, so to speak, of her soul - is entirely woven from threads of Holy Scripture, threads drawn from the Word of God. Here we see how completely at home Mary is with the Word of God, with ease she moves in and out of it. She speaks and thinks with the Word of God; the Word of God becomes her word, and her word issues from the Word of God. Here we see how her thoughts are attuned to the thoughts of God, how her will is one with the will of God. Since Mary is completely imbued with the Word of God, she is able to become the Mother of the Word Incarnate. Finally, Mary is a woman who loves. How could it be otherwise? As a believer who in faith thinks with God's thoughts and wills with God's will, she cannot fail to be a woman who loves. We sense this in her quiet gestures, as recounted by the infancy narratives in the Gospel. We see it in the delicacy with which she recognises the need of the spouses at Cana and makes it known to Jesus. We see it in the humility with which she recedes into the background during Jesus' public life, knowing that the Son must establish a new family and that the Mother's hour will come only with the Cross, which will be Jesus' true hour (cf. *Jn* 2:4; 13:1). When the disciples flee,

Mary will remain beneath the Cross (cf. *Jn* 19:25-27); later, at the hour of Pentecost, it will be they who gather around her as they wait for the Holy Spirit (cf. *Ac* 1:14).

42. The lives of the saints are not limited to their earthly biographies but also include their being and working in God after death. In the saints one thing becomes clear: those who draw near to God do not withdraw from men, but rather become truly close to them. In no one do we see this more clearly than in Mary. The words addressed by the crucified Lord to his disciple - to John and through him to all disciples of Jesus: "Behold, your mother!" (*Jn* 19:27) - are fulfilled anew in every generation. Mary has truly become the Mother of all believers. Men and women of every time and place have recourse to her motherly kindness and her virginal purity and grace, in all their needs and aspirations, their joys and sorrows, their moments of loneliness and their common endeavours. They constantly experience the gift of her goodness and the unfailing love which she pours out from the depths of her heart. The testimonials of gratitude, offered to her from every continent and culture, are a recognition of that pure love which is not self-seeking but simply benevolent. At the same time, the devotion of the faithful shows an infallible intuition of how such love is possible: it becomes so as a result of the most intimate union with God, through which the soul is totally pervaded by him - a condition which enables those who have drunk from the fountain of God's love to become in their turn a fountain from which "flow rivers of living water" (*Jn* 7:38). Mary, Virgin and Mother, shows us what love is and whence it draws its origin and its constantly renewed power. To her we entrust the Church and her mission in the service of love:

Holy Mary, Mother of God,
you have given the world its true light,
Jesus, your Son - the Son of God.
You abandoned yourself completely
to God's call
and thus became a wellspring
of the goodness which flows forth from him.
Show us Jesus. Lead us to him.
Teach us to know and love him,
so that we too can become
capable of true love
and be fountains of living water
in the midst of a thirsting world.

Given in Rome, at Saint Peter's, on 25th December, the Solemnity of the Nativity of the Lord, in the year 2005, the first of my Pontificate.

BENEDICTUS PP. XVI

ENCYCLICAL LETTER

SPE SALVI

OF THE SUPREME PONTIFF

BENEDICT XVI

TO THE BISHOPS
PRIESTS AND DEACONS
MEN AND WOMEN RELIGIOUS
AND ALL THE LAY FAITHFUL

ON CHRISTIAN HOPE

Contents

Introduction

1. "*SPE SALVI facti sumus*" - in hope we were saved, says Saint Paul to the Romans, and likewise to us (*Rm* 8:24). According to the Christian faith, "redemption" - salvation - is not simply a given. Redemption is offered to us in the sense that we have been given hope, trustworthy hope, by virtue of which we can face our present: the present, even if it is arduous, can be lived and accepted if it leads towards a goal, if we can be sure of this goal, and if this goal is great enough to justify the effort of the journey. Now the question immediately arises: what sort of hope could ever justify the statement that, on the basis of that hope and simply because it exists, we are redeemed? And what sort of certainty is involved here?

Faith is Hope

2. Before turning our attention to these timely questions, we must listen a little more closely to the Bible's testimony on hope. "Hope", in fact, is a key word in Biblical faith - so much so that in several passages the words "faith" and "hope" seem interchangeable. Thus the *Letter to the Hebrews* closely links the "fullness of faith" (10:22) to "the confession of our hope without wavering" (10:23). Likewise, when the *First Letter of Peter* exhorts Christians to be always ready to give an answer concerning the *logos* - the meaning and the reason - of their hope (cf. 3:15), "hope" is equivalent to "faith". We see how decisively the self-understanding of the early Christians was shaped by their having received the gift of a trustworthy hope, when we compare the Christian life with life prior to faith, or with the situation of the followers of other religions. Paul reminds the Ephesians that before their encounter with Christ they were "without hope and without God in the world" (*Ep* 2:12). Of course he knew they had had gods, he knew they had had a religion, but their gods had proved questionable, and no hope emerged from their contradictory myths. Notwithstanding their gods, they were

55

"without God" and consequently found themselves in a dark world, facing a dark future. *In nihil ab nihilo quam cito recedimus* (How quickly we fall back from nothing to nothing):[1] so says an epitaph of that period. In this phrase we see in no uncertain terms the point Paul was making. In the same vein he says to the Thessalonians: you must not "grieve as others do who have no hope" (1 *Th* 4:13). Here too we see as a distinguishing mark of Christians the fact that they have a future: it is not that they know the details of what awaits them, but they know in general terms that their life will not end in emptiness. Only when the future is certain as a positive reality does it become possible to live the present as well. So now we can say: Christianity was not only "good news" - the communication of a hitherto unknown content. In our language we would say: the Christian message was not only "informative" but "performative". That means: the Gospel is not merely a communication of things that can be known - it is one that makes things happen and is life-changing. The dark door of time, of the future, has been thrown open. The one who has hope lives differently; the one who hopes has been granted the gift of a new life.

3. Yet at this point a question arises: in what does this hope consist which, as hope, is "redemption"? The essence of the answer is given in the phrase from the *Letter to the Ephesians* quoted above: the Ephesians, before their encounter with Christ, were without hope because they were "without God in the world". To come to know God - the true God - means to receive hope. We who have always lived with the Christian concept of God, and have grown accustomed to it, have almost ceased to notice that we possess the hope that ensues from a real encounter with this God. The example of a saint of our time can to some degree help us understand what it means to have a real encounter with this God for the first time. I am thinking of the African Josephine Bakhita, canonised by Pope John Paul II. She was born around 1869 - she herself did not know the precise date - in Darfur in Sudan. At the age of nine, she was kidnapped by slave-traders, beaten till she bled, and sold five

---

[1] *Corpus Inscriptionum Latinarum* VI, no. 26003.

times in the slave-markets of Sudan. Eventually she found herself working as a slave for the mother and the wife of a general, and there she was flogged every day till she bled; as a result of this she bore 144 scars throughout her life. Finally, in 1882, she was bought by an Italian merchant for the Italian consul Callisto Legnani, who returned to Italy as the Mahdists advanced. Here, after the terrifying "masters" who had owned her up to that point, Bakhita came to know a totally different kind of "master" - in Venetian dialect, which she was now learning, she used the name "*paron*" for the living God, the God of Jesus Christ. Up to that time she had known only masters who despised and maltreated her, or at best considered her a useful slave. Now, however, she heard that there is a "*paron*" above all masters, the Lord of all lords, and that this Lord is good, goodness in person. She came to know that this Lord even knew her, that he had created her - that he actually loved her. She too was loved, and by none other than the supreme "*Paron*", before whom all other masters are themselves no more than lowly servants. She was known and loved and she was awaited. What is more, this master had himself accepted the destiny of being flogged and now he was waiting for her "at the Father's right hand". Now she had "hope" - no longer simply the modest hope of finding masters who would be less cruel, but the great hope: "I am definitively loved and whatever happens to me - I am awaited by this Love. And so my life is good." Through the knowledge of this hope she was "redeemed", no longer a slave, but a free child of God. She understood what Paul meant when he reminded the Ephesians that previously they were without hope and without God in the world - without hope *because* without God. Hence, when she was about to be taken back to Sudan, Bakhita refused; she did not wish to be separated again from her "*Paron*". On 9th January 1890, she was baptised and confirmed and received her first Holy Communion from the hands of the Patriarch of Venice. On 8th December 1896, in Verona, she took her vows in the Congregation of the Canossian Sisters and from that time onwards, besides her work in the sacristy and in the porter's lodge at the convent, she made several journeys round Italy in order to promote the missions: the liberation that she had received through her encounter with the God of Jesus Christ, she felt she had to extend, it had to be handed on to others, to the greatest possible number of people. The hope born in her which had "redeemed" her she could not keep to herself; this hope had to reach many, to reach everybody.

The concept of faith-based hope in the New Testament and the early Church

4. We have raised the question: can our encounter with the God who in Christ has shown us his face and opened his heart be for us too not just "informative" but "performative" - that is to say, can it change our lives, so that we know we are redeemed through the hope that it expresses? Before attempting to answer the question, let us return once more to the early Church. It is not difficult to realise that the experience of the African slave-girl Bakhita was also the experience of many in the period of nascent Christianity who were beaten and condemned to slavery. Christianity did not bring a message of social revolution like that of the ill-fated Spartacus, whose struggle led to so much bloodshed. Jesus was not Spartacus, he was not engaged in a fight for political liberation like Barabbas or Bar Kochba. Jesus, who himself died on the Cross, brought something totally different: an encounter with the Lord of all lords, an encounter with the living God and thus an encounter with a hope stronger than the sufferings of slavery, a hope which therefore transformed life and the world from within. What was new here can be seen with the utmost clarity in Saint Paul's *Letter to Philemon*. This is a very personal letter, which Paul wrote from prison and entrusted to the runaway slave Onesimus for his master, Philemon. Yes, Paul is sending the slave back to the master from whom he had fled, not ordering but asking: "I appeal to you for my child...whose father I have become in my imprisonment...I am sending him back to you, sending my very heart...perhaps this is why he was parted from you for a while, that you might have him back for ever, no longer as a slave but more than a slave, as a beloved

brother..." (*Phm* 10-16). Those who, as far as their civil status is concerned, stand in relation to one another as masters and slaves, inasmuch as they are members of the one Church have become brothers and sisters - this is how Christians addressed one another. By virtue of their Baptism they had been reborn, they had been given to drink of the same Spirit and they received the Body of the Lord together, alongside one another. Even if external structures remained unaltered, this changed society from within. When the *Letter to the Hebrews* says that Christians here on earth do not have a permanent homeland, but seek one which lies in the future (cf. *Heb* 11:13-16; *Ph* 3:20), this does not mean for one moment that they live only for the future: present society is recognised by Christians as an exile; they belong to a new society which is the goal of their common pilgrimage and which is anticipated in the course of that pilgrimage.

5. We must add a further point of view. The *First Letter to the Corinthians* (1:18-31) tells us that many of the early Christians belonged to the lower social strata, and precisely for this reason were open to the experience of new hope, as we saw in the example of Bakhita. Yet from the beginning there were also conversions in the aristocratic and cultured circles, since they too were living "without hope and without God in the world". Myth had lost its credibility; the Roman State religion had become fossilised into simple ceremony which was scrupulously carried out, but by then it was merely "political religion". Philosophical rationalism had confined the gods within the realm of unreality. The Divine was seen in various ways in cosmic forces, but a God to whom one could pray did not exist. Paul illustrates the essential problem of the religion of that time quite accurately when he contrasts life "according to Christ" with life under the dominion of the "elemental spirits of the universe" (*Col* 2:8). In this regard a text by Saint Gregory Nazianzen is enlightening. He says that at the very moment when the Magi, guided by the star, adored Christ the new king, astrology came to an end, because the stars were now moving

in the orbit determined by Christ.[2] This scene, in fact, overturns the world-view of that time, which in a different way has become fashionable once again today. It is not the elemental spirits of the universe, the laws of matter, which ultimately govern the world and mankind, but a personal God governs the stars, that is, the universe; it is not the laws of matter and of evolution that have the final say, but reason, will, love - a Person. And if we know this Person and he knows us, then truly the inexorable power of material elements no longer has the last word; we are not slaves of the universe and of its laws, we are free. In ancient times, honest enquiring minds were aware of this. Heaven is not empty. Life is not a simple product of laws and the randomness of matter, but within everything and at the same time above everything, there is a personal will, there is a Spirit who in Jesus has revealed himself as Love.[3]

6. The sarcophagi of the early Christian era illustrate this concept visually - in the context of death, in the face of which the question concerning life's meaning becomes unavoidable. The figure of Christ is interpreted on ancient sarcophagi principally by two images: the philosopher and the shepherd. Philosophy at that time was not generally seen as a difficult academic discipline, as it is today. Rather, the philosopher was someone who knew how to teach the essential art: the art of being authentically human - the art of living and dying. To be sure, it had long since been realised that many of the people who went around pretending to be philosophers, teachers of life, were just charlatans who made money through their words, while having nothing to say about real life. All the more, then, the true philosopher who really did know how to point out the path of life was highly sought after. Towards the end of the third century, on the sarcophagus of a child in Rome, we find for the first time, in the context of the resurrection of Lazarus, the figure of Christ as the true philosopher, holding the Gospel in one hand and the philosopher's travelling staff in the other. With his staff, he conquers death; the Gospel brings the truth that itinerant

2 Cf. *Dogmatic Poems*, V, 53-64: *PG* 37, 428-429.
3 Cf. *Catechism of the Catholic Church*, 1817-1821.

philosophers had searched for in vain. In this image, which then became a common feature of sarcophagus art for a long time, we see clearly what both educated and simple people found in Christ: he tells us who man truly is and what a man must do in order to be truly human. He shows us the way, and this way is the truth. He himself is both the way and the truth, and therefore he is also the life which all of us are seeking. He also shows us the way beyond death; only someone able to do this is a true teacher of life. The same thing becomes visible in the image of the shepherd. As in the representation of the philosopher, so too through the figure of the shepherd the early Church could identify with existing models of Roman art. There the shepherd was generally an expression of the dream of a tranquil and simple life, for which the people, amid the confusion of the big cities, felt a certain longing. Now the image was read as part of a new scenario which gave it a deeper content: "The Lord is my shepherd: I shall not want... Even though I walk through the valley of the shadow of death, I fear no evil, because you are with me..." (*Ps* 23 [22]:1,4). The true shepherd is one who knows even the path that passes through the valley of death; one who walks with me even on the path of final solitude, where no one can accompany me, guiding me through: he himself has walked this path, he has descended into the kingdom of death, he has conquered death, and he has returned to accompany us now and to give us the certainty that, together with him, we can find a way through. The realisation that there is One who even in death accompanies me, and with his "rod and his staff comforts me", so that "I fear no evil" (cf. *Ps* 23 [22]:4) - this was the new "hope" that arose over the life of believers.

7. We must return once more to the New Testament. In the eleventh chapter of the *Letter to the Hebrews* (v. 1) we find a kind of definition of faith which closely links this virtue with hope. Ever since the Reformation there has been a dispute among exegetes over the central word of this phrase, but today a way towards a common interpretation seems to be opening up once more. For the time being I shall leave this central word untranslated. The sentence therefore

reads as follows: "Faith is the *hypostasis* of things hoped for; the proof of things not seen." For the Fathers and for the theologians of the Middle Ages, it was clear that the Greek word *hypostasis* was to be rendered in Latin with the term *substantia*. The Latin translation of the text produced at the time of the early Church therefore reads: *Est autem fides sperandarum substantia rerum, argumentum non apparentium* - faith is the "substance" of things hoped for; the proof of things not seen. Saint Thomas Aquinas,[4] using the terminology of the philosophical tradition to which he belonged, explains it as follows: faith is a *habitus*, that is, a stable disposition of the spirit, through which eternal life takes root in us and reason is led to consent to what it does not see. The concept of "substance" is therefore modified in the sense that through faith, in a tentative way, or as we might say "in embryo" - and thus according to the "substance" - there are already present in us the things that are hoped for: the whole, true life. And precisely because the thing itself is already present, this presence of what is to come also creates certainty: this "thing" which must come is not yet visible in the external world (it does not "appear"), but because of the fact that, as an initial and dynamic reality, we carry it within us, a certain perception of it has even now come into existence. To Luther, who was not particularly fond of the *Letter to the Hebrews*, the concept of "substance", in the context of his view of faith, meant nothing. For this reason he understood the term *hypostasis/substance* not in the objective sense (of a reality present within us), but in the subjective sense, as an expression of an interior attitude, and so, naturally, he also had to understand the term *argumentum* as a disposition of the subject. In the twentieth century this interpretation became prevalent - at least in Germany - in Catholic exegesis too, so that the ecumenical translation into German of the New Testament, approved by the Bishops, reads as follows: *Glaube aber ist: Feststehen in dem, was man erhofft, Überzeugtsein von dem, was man nicht sieht* (faith is: standing firm in what one hopes, being convinced of what one does not see). This in itself is not incorrect, but it is not the meaning of the text, because the Greek term used (*elenchos*) does not have

4 *Summa Theologiae*, II-IIae, q. 4, a. 1.

the subjective sense of "conviction" but the objective sense of "proof". Rightly, therefore, recent Protestant exegesis has arrived at a different interpretation: "Yet there can be no question but that this classical Protestant understanding is untenable."[5] Faith is not merely a personal reaching out towards things to come that are still totally absent: it gives us something. It gives us even now something of the reality we are waiting for, and this present reality constitutes for us a "proof" of the things that are still unseen. Faith draws the future into the present, so that it is no longer simply a "not yet". The fact that this future exists changes the present; the present is touched by the future reality, and thus the things of the future spill over into those of the present and those of the present into those of the future.

8. This explanation is further strengthened and related to daily life if we consider verse 34 of the tenth chapter of the *Letter to the Hebrews*, which is linked by vocabulary and content to this definition of hope-filled faith and prepares the way for it. Here the author speaks to believers who have undergone the experience of persecution and he says to them: "you had compassion on the prisoners, and you joyfully accepted the plundering of your property (*hyparchonton* - Vg. *bonorum*), since you knew that you yourselves had a better possession (*hyparxin* - Vg. *substantiam*) and an abiding one." *Hyparchonta* refers to property, to what in earthly life constitutes the means of support, indeed the basis, the "substance" for life, what we depend upon. This "substance", life's normal source of security, has been taken away from Christians in the course of persecution. They have stood firm, though, because they considered this material substance to be of little account. They could abandon it because they had found a better "basis" for their existence - a basis that abides, that no one can take away. We must not overlook the link between these two types of "substance", between means of support or material basis and the word of faith as the "basis", the "substance" that endures. Faith gives life a new basis, a new foundation on which we can stand, one which

---

[5] H. Köster in *Theological Dictionary of the New Testament* VIII (1972), p. 586.

relativises the habitual foundation, the reliability of material income. A new freedom is created with regard to this habitual foundation of life, which only *appears* to be capable of providing support, although this is obviously not to deny its normal meaning. This new freedom, the awareness of the new "substance" which we have been given, is revealed not only in martyrdom, in which people resist the overbearing power of ideology and its political organs and, by their death, renew the world. Above all, it is seen in the great acts of renunciation, from the monks of ancient times to Saint Francis of Assisi and those of our contemporaries who enter modern religious Institutes and movements and leave everything for love of Christ, so as to bring to men and women the faith and love of Christ, and to help those who are suffering in body and spirit. In their case, the new "substance" has proved to be a genuine "substance"; from the hope of these people who have been touched by Christ, hope has arisen for others who were living in darkness and without hope. In their case, it has been demonstrated that this new life truly possesses and is "substance" that calls forth life for others. For us who contemplate these figures, their way of acting and living is *de facto* a "proof" that the things to come, the promise of Christ, are not only a reality that we await, but a real presence: he is truly the "philosopher" and the "shepherd" who shows us what life is and where it is to be found.

9. In order to understand more deeply this reflection on the two types of substance - *hypostasis* and *hyparchonta* - and on the two approaches to life expressed by these terms, we must continue with a brief consideration of two words pertinent to the discussion which can be found in the tenth chapter of the *Letter to the Hebrews*. I refer to the words *hypomone* (10:36) and *hypostole* (10:39). *Hypomone* is normally translated as "patience" - perseverance, constancy. Knowing how to wait, while patiently enduring trials, is necessary for the believer to be able to "receive what is promised" (10:36). In the religious context of ancient Judaism, this word was used expressly for the expectation of God which was characteristic of Israel, for their persevering faithfulness to God on the basis of the

certainty of the Covenant in a world which contradicts God. Thus the word indicates a lived hope, a life based on the certainty of hope. In the New Testament this expectation of God, this standing with God, takes on a new significance: in Christ, God has revealed himself. He has already communicated to us the "substance" of things to come, and thus the expectation of God acquires a new certainty. It is the expectation of things to come from the perspective of a present that is already given. It is a looking-forward in Christ's presence, with Christ who is present, to the perfecting of his Body, to his definitive coming. The word *hypostole*, on the other hand, means shrinking back through lack of courage to speak openly and frankly a truth that may be dangerous. Hiding through a spirit of fear leads to "destruction" (*Heb* 10:39). "God did not give us a spirit of timidity but a spirit of power and love and selfcontrol" - that, by contrast, is the beautiful way in which the *Second Letter to Timothy* (1:7) describes the fundamental attitude of the Christian.

Eternal life - what is it?

10. We have spoken thus far of faith and hope in the New Testament and in early Christianity; yet it has always been clear that we are referring not only to the past: the entire reflection concerns living and dying in general, and therefore it also concerns us here and now. So now we must ask explicitly: is the Christian faith also for us today a life-changing and life-sustaining hope? Is it "performative" for us - is it a message which shapes our life in a new way, or is it just "information" which, in the meantime, we have set aside and which now seems to us to have been superseded by more recent information? In the search for an answer, I would like to begin with the classical form of the dialogue with which the rite of Baptism expressed the reception of an infant into the community of believers and the infant's rebirth in Christ. First of all the priest asked what name the parents had chosen for the child, and then he continued with the question: "What do you ask of the Church?" Answer: "Faith". "And what does faith give you?" "Eternal life". According to this dialogue, the parents were seeking access to the faith for their child, communion with believers,

Spe Salvi

because they saw in faith the key to "eternal life". Today as in the past, this is what being baptised, becoming Christians, is all about: it is not just an act of socialisation within the community, not simply a welcome into the Church. The parents expect more for the one to be baptised: they expect that faith, which includes the corporeal nature of the Church and her sacraments, will give life to their child - eternal life. Faith is the substance of hope. But then the question arises: do we really want this - to live eternally? Perhaps many people reject the faith today simply because they do not find the prospect of eternal life attractive. What they desire is not eternal life at all, but this present life, for which faith in eternal life seems something of an impediment. To continue living for ever - endlessly - appears more like a curse than a gift. Death, admittedly, one would wish to postpone for as long as possible. But to live always, without end - this, all things considered, can only be monotonous and ultimately unbearable. This is precisely the point made, for example, by Saint Ambrose, one of the Church Fathers, in the funeral discourse for his deceased brother Satyrus: "Death was not part of nature; it became part of nature. God did not decree death from the beginning; he prescribed it as a remedy. Human life, because of sin...began to experience the burden of wretchedness in unremitting labour and unbearable sorrow. There had to be a limit to its evils; death had to restore what life had forfeited. Without the assistance of grace, immortality is more of a burden than a blessing."[6] A little earlier, Ambrose had said: "Death is, then, no cause for mourning, for it is the cause of mankind's salvation."[7]

11. Whatever precisely Saint Ambrose may have meant by these words, it is true that to eliminate death or to postpone it more or less indefinitely would place the earth and humanity in an impossible situation, and even for the individual would bring no benefit. Obviously there is a contradiction in our attitude, which points to an inner contradiction in our very existence. On the one hand, we do not want to die; above all, those who love us do not want us to die. Yet on the other hand, neither do we want to continue living

---

[6] *De excessu fratris sui Satyri*, II, 47: *CSEL* 73, 274.
[7] *Ibid.*, II, 46: *CSEL* 73, 273.

indefinitely, nor was the earth created with that in view. So what do we really want? Our paradoxical attitude gives rise to a deeper question: what in fact is "life"? And what does "eternity" really mean? There are moments when it suddenly seems clear to us: yes, this is what true "life" is - this is what it should be like. Besides, what we call "life" in our everyday language is not real "life" at all. Saint Augustine, in the extended letter on prayer which he addressed to Proba, a wealthy Roman widow and mother of three consuls, once wrote this: ultimately we want only one thing - "the blessed life", the life which is simply life, simply "happiness". In the final analysis, there is nothing else that we ask for in prayer. Our journey has no other goal - it is about this alone. But then Augustine also says: looking more closely, we have no idea what we ultimately desire, what we would really like. We do not know this reality at all; even in those moments when we think we can reach out and touch it, it eludes us. "We do not know what we should pray for as we ought," he says, quoting Saint Paul (*Rm* 8:26). All we know is that it is not this. Yet in not knowing, we know that this reality must exist. "There is therefore in us a certain learned ignorance (*docta ignorantia*), so to speak", he writes. We do not know what we would really like; we do not know this "true life"; and yet we know that there must be something we do not know towards which we feel driven.[8]

12. I think that in this very precise and permanently valid way, Augustine is describing man's essential situation, the situation that gives rise to all his contradictions and hopes. In some way we want life itself, true life, untouched even by death; yet at the same time we do not know the thing towards which we feel driven. We cannot stop reaching out for it, and yet we know that all we can experience or accomplish is not what we yearn for. This unknown "thing" is the true "hope" which drives us, and at the same time the fact that it is unknown is the cause of all forms of despair and also of all efforts, whether positive or destructive, directed towards worldly authenticity and human authenticity. The term "eternal life" is intended to give a

---

[8] Cf. Ep. 130 *Ad Probam* 14, 25-15, 28: *CSEL* 44, 68-73.

name to this known "unknown". Inevitably it is an inadequate term that creates confusion. "Eternal", in fact, suggests to us the idea of something interminable, and this frightens us; "life" makes us think of the life that we know and love and do not want to lose, even though very often it brings more toil than satisfaction, so that while on the one hand we desire it, on the other hand we do not want it. To imagine ourselves outside the temporality that imprisons us and in some way to sense that eternity is not an unending succession of days in the calendar, but something more like the supreme moment of satisfaction, in which totality embraces us and we embrace totality - this we can only attempt. It would be like plunging into the ocean of infinite love, a moment in which time - the before and after - no longer exists. We can only attempt to grasp the idea that such a moment is life in the full sense, a plunging ever anew into the vastness of being, in which we are simply overwhelmed with joy. This is how Jesus expresses it in *Saint John's Gospel*: "I will see you again and your hearts will rejoice, and no one will take your joy from you" (16:22). We must think along these lines if we want to understand the object of Christian hope, to understand what it is that our faith, our being with Christ, leads us to expect.[9]

Is Christian hope individualistic?

13. In the course of their history, Christians have tried to express this "knowing without knowing" by means of figures that can be represented, and they have developed images of "Heaven" which remain far removed from what, after all, can only be known negatively, via unknowing. All these attempts at the representation of hope have given to many people, down the centuries, the incentive to live by faith and hence also to abandon their *hyparchonta*, the material substance for their lives. The author of the *Letter to the Hebrews*, in the eleventh chapter, outlined a kind of history of those who live in hope and of their journeying, a history which stretches from the time of Abel into the author's own day. This type of hope has been subjected to an increasingly harsh critique

---

[9] Cf. *Catechism of the Catholic Church*, 1025.

in modern times: it is dismissed as pure individualism, a way of abandoning the world to its misery and taking refuge in a private form of eternal salvation. Henri de Lubac, in the introduction to his seminal book *Catholicisme. Aspects sociaux du dogme*, assembled some characteristic articulations of this viewpoint, one of which is worth quoting: "Should I have found joy? No...only *my* joy, and that is something wildly different... The joy of Jesus can be personal. It can belong to a single man and he is saved. He is at peace...now and always, but he is alone. The isolation of this joy does not trouble him. On the contrary: he is the chosen one! In his blessedness he passes through the battlefields with a rose in his hand."[10]

14. Against this, drawing upon the vast range of patristic theology, de Lubac was able to demonstrate that salvation has always been considered a "social" reality. Indeed, the *Letter to the Hebrews* speaks of a "city" (cf. 11:10, 16; 12:22; 13:14) and therefore of communal salvation. Consistently with this view, sin is understood by the Fathers as the destruction of the unity of the human race, as fragmentation and division. Babel, the place where languages were confused, the place of separation, is seen to be an expression of what sin fundamentally is. Hence "redemption" appears as the reestablishment of unity, in which we come together once more in a union that begins to take shape in the world community of believers. We need not concern ourselves here with all the texts in which the social character of hope appears. Let us concentrate on the *Letter to Proba* in which Augustine tries to illustrate to some degree this "known unknown" that we seek. His point of departure is simply the expression "blessed life". Then he quotes *Psalm* 144 [143]:15: "Blessed is the people whose God is the Lord." And he continues: "In order to be numbered among this people and attain to...everlasting life with God, 'the end of the commandment is charity that issues from a pure heart and a good conscience and sincere faith' (1 *Tm* 1:5)."[11] This real life, towards which we try to

---

[10] Jean Giono, *Les vraies richesses* (1936), Preface, Paris 1992, pp. 18-20; quoted in Henri de Lubac, *Catholicisme. Aspects sociaux du dogme*, Paris 1983, p. VII.
[11] Ep. 130 *Ad Probam* 13, 24: *CSEL* 44, 67.

reach out again and again, is linked to a lived union with a "people", and for each individual it can only be attained within this "we". It presupposes that we escape from the prison of our "I", because only in the openness of this universal subject does our gaze open out to the source of joy, to love itself - to God.

15. While this community-oriented vision of the "blessed life" is certainly directed beyond the present world, as such it also has to do with the building up of this world - in very different ways, according to the historical context and the possibilities offered or excluded thereby. At the time of Augustine, the incursions of new peoples were threatening the cohesion of the world, where hitherto there had been a certain guarantee of law and of living in a juridically ordered society; at that time, then, it was a matter of strengthening the basic foundations of this peaceful societal existence, in order to survive in a changed world. Let us now consider a more or less randomly chosen episode from the Middle Ages, that serves in many respects to illustrate what we have been saying. It was commonly thought that monasteries were places of flight from the world (*contemptus mundi*) and of withdrawal from responsibility for the world, in search of private salvation. Bernard of Clairvaux, who inspired a multitude of young people to enter the monasteries of his reformed Order, had quite a different perspective on this. In his view, monks perform a task for the whole Church and hence also for the world. He uses many images to illustrate the responsibility that monks have towards the entire body of the Church, and indeed towards humanity; he applies to them the words of pseudo-Rufinus: "The human race lives thanks to a few; were it not for them, the world would perish...".[12] Contemplatives - *contemplantes* - must become agricultural labourers - *laborantes* - he says. The nobility of work, which Christianity inherited from Judaism, had already been expressed in the monastic rules of Augustine and Benedict. Bernard takes up this idea again. The young noblemen who flocked to his monasteries had to engage in manual labour. In fact Bernard explicitly states that not even the monastery can restore Paradise, but he maintains that, as a place

---

[12] *Sententiae* III, 118: *CCL* 6/2, 215.

of practical and spiritual "tilling the soil", it must prepare the new Paradise. A wild plot of forest land is rendered fertile - and in the process, the trees of pride are felled, whatever weeds may be growing inside souls are pulled up, and the ground is thereby prepared so that bread for body and soul can flourish.[13] Are we not perhaps seeing once again, in the light of current history, that no positive world order can prosper where souls are overgrown?

The transformation of Christian faith-hope in the modern age

16. How could the idea have developed that Jesus's message is narrowly individualistic and aimed only at each person singly? How did we arrive at this interpretation of the "salvation of the soul" as a flight from responsibility for the whole, and how did we come to conceive the Christian project as a selfish search for salvation which rejects the idea of serving others? In order to find an answer to this we must take a look at the foundations of the modern age. These appear with particular clarity in the thought of Francis Bacon. That a new era emerged - through the discovery of America and the new technical achievements that had made this development possible - is undeniable. But what is the basis of this new era? It is the new correlation of experiment and method that enables man to arrive at an interpretation of nature in conformity with its laws and thus finally to achieve "the triumph of art over nature" (*victoria cursus artis super naturam*).[14] The novelty - according to Bacon's vision - lies in a new correlation between science and praxis. This is also given a theological application: the new correlation between science and praxis would mean that the dominion over creation - given to man by God and lost through original sin - would be reestablished.[15]

---

[13] Cf. *ibid.* III, 71: *CCL* 6/2, 107-108.

[14] *Novum Organum* I, 117.

[15] Cf. *ibid.* I, 129.

17. Anyone who reads and reflects on these statements attentively will recognise that a disturbing step has been taken: up to that time, the recovery of what man had lost through the expulsion from Paradise was expected from faith in Jesus Christ: herein lay "redemption". Now, this "redemption", the restoration of the lost "Paradise" is no longer expected from faith, but from the newly discovered link between science and praxis. It is not that faith is simply denied; rather it is displaced onto another level - that of purely private and other-worldly affairs - and at the same time it becomes somehow irrelevant for the world. This programmatic vision has determined the trajectory of modern times and it also shapes the present-day crisis of faith which is essentially a crisis of Christian hope. Thus hope too, in Bacon, acquires a new form. Now it is called: *faith in progress*. For Bacon, it is clear that the recent spate of discoveries and inventions is just the beginning; through the interplay of science and praxis, totally new discoveries will follow, a totally new world will emerge, the kingdom of man.[16] He even put forward a vision of foreseeable inventions - including the aeroplane and the submarine. As the ideology of progress developed further, joy at visible advances in human potential remained a continuing confirmation of *faith in progress* as such.

18. At the same time, two categories become increasingly central to the idea of progress: reason and freedom. Progress is primarily associated with the growing dominion of reason, and this reason is obviously considered to be a force of good and a force for good. Progress is the overcoming of all forms of dependency - it is progress towards perfect freedom. Likewise freedom is seen purely as a promise, in which man becomes more and more fully himself. In both concepts - freedom and reason - there is a political aspect. The kingdom of reason, in fact, is expected as the new condition of the human race once it has attained total freedom. The political conditions of such a kingdom of reason and freedom, however, appear at first sight somewhat ill defined. Reason and freedom seem to guarantee by themselves, by virtue of their intrinsic goodness,

[16] Cf. *New Atlantis*.

a new and perfect human community. The two key concepts of "reason" and "freedom", however, were tacitly interpreted as being in conflict with the shackles of faith and of the Church as well as those of the political structures of the period. Both concepts therefore contain a revolutionary potential of enormous explosive force.

19. We must look briefly at the two essential stages in the political realisation of this hope, because they are of great importance for the development of Christian hope, for a proper understanding of it and of the reasons for its persistence. First there is the French Revolution - an attempt to establish the rule of reason and freedom as a political reality. To begin with, the Europe of the Enlightenment looked on with fascination at these events, but then, as they developed, had cause to reflect anew on reason and freedom. A good illustration of these two phases in the reception of events in France is found in two essays by Immanuel Kant in which he reflects on what had taken place. In 1792 he wrote *Der Sieg des guten Prinzips über das böse und die Gründung eines Reiches Gottes auf Erden* ("The Victory of the Good over the Evil Principle and the Founding of a Kingdom of God on Earth"). In this text he says the following: "The gradual transition of ecclesiastical faith to the exclusive sovereignty of pure religious faith is the coming of the Kingdom of God."[17] He also tells us that revolutions can accelerate this transition from ecclesiastical faith to rational faith. The "Kingdom of God" proclaimed by Jesus receives a new definition here and takes on a new mode of presence; a new "imminent expectation", so to speak, comes into existence: the "Kingdom of God" arrives where "ecclesiastical faith" is vanquished and superseded by "religious faith", that is to say, by simple rational faith. In 1795, in the text *Das Ende aller Dinge* ("The End of All Things") a changed image appears. Now Kant considers the possibility that as well as the natural end of all things there may be another that is unnatural, a perverse end. He writes in this connection: "If Christianity should one day cease to be worthy of love...then the prevailing mode in human thought would be rejection and opposition to it; and the Antichrist...would

---

[17] In *Werke* IV, ed. W. Weischedel (1956), p. 777.

73

begin his - albeit short - regime (presumably based on fear and self-interest); but then, because Christianity, though destined to be the world religion, would not in fact be favoured by destiny to become so, then, in a moral respect, this could lead to the (perverted) end of all things."[18]

20. The nineteenth century held fast to its faith in progress as the new form of human hope, and it continued to consider reason and freedom as the guiding stars to be followed along the path of hope. Nevertheless, the increasingly rapid advance of technical development and the industrialisation connected with it soon gave rise to an entirely new social situation: there emerged a class of industrial workers and the so-called "industrial proletariat", whose dreadful living conditions Friedrich Engels described alarmingly in 1845. For his readers, the conclusion is clear: this cannot continue; a change is necessary. Yet the change would shake up and overturn the entire structure of bourgeois society. After the bourgeois revolution of 1789, the time had come for a new, proletarian revolution: progress could not simply continue in small, linear steps. A revolutionary leap was needed. Karl Marx took up the rallying call, and applied his incisive language and intellect to the task of launching this major new and, as he thought, definitive step in history towards salvation - towards what Kant had described as the "Kingdom of God". Once the truth of the hereafter had been rejected, it would then be a question of establishing the truth of the here and now. The critique of Heaven is transformed into the critique of earth, the critique of theology into the critique of politics. Progress towards the better, towards the definitively good world, no longer comes simply from science but from politics - from a scientifically conceived politics that recognises the structure of history and society and thus points out the road towards revolution, towards all-encompassing change. With great precision, albeit with a certain onesided bias, Marx described the situation of his time, and with great analytical skill he spelled out the paths leading to revolution - and not only theoretically: by means of the Communist

---

[18] I. Kant, *Das Ende aller Dinge*, in *Werke* VI, ed. W. Weischedel (1964), p. 190.

Party that came into being from the Communist Manifesto of 1848, he set it in motion. His promise, owing to the acuteness of his analysis and his clear indication of the means for radical change, was and still remains an endless source of fascination. Real revolution followed, in the most radical way in Russia.

21. Together with the victory of the revolution, though, Marx's fundamental error also became evident. He showed precisely how to overthrow the existing order, but he did not say how matters should proceed thereafter. He simply presumed that with the expropriation of the ruling class, with the fall of political power and the socialisation of means of production, the new Jerusalem would be realised. Then, indeed, all contradictions would be resolved, man and the world would finally sort themselves out. Then everything would be able to proceed by itself along the right path, because everything would belong to everyone and all would desire the best for one another. Thus, having accomplished the revolution, Lenin must have realised that the writings of the master gave no indication as to how to proceed. True, Marx had spoken of the interim phase of the dictatorship of the proletariat as a necessity which in time would automatically become redundant. This "intermediate phase" we know all too well, and we also know how it then developed, not ushering in a perfect world, but leaving behind a trail of appalling destruction. Marx not only omitted to work out how this new world would be organised - which should, of course, have been unnecessary. His silence on this matter follows logically from his chosen approach. His error lay deeper. He forgot that man always remains man. He forgot man and he forgot man's freedom. He forgot that freedom always remains also freedom for evil. He thought that once the economy had been put right, everything would automatically be put right. His real error is materialism: man, in fact, is not merely the product of economic conditions, and it is not possible to redeem him purely from the outside by creating a favourable economic environment.

22. Again, we find ourselves facing the question: what may we hope? A self-critique of modernity is needed in dialogue with Christianity and its concept of hope. In this dialogue Christians too, in the context of their knowledge and experience, must learn anew in what their hope truly consists, what they have to offer to the world and what they cannot offer. Flowing into this self-critique of the modern age there also has to be a self-critique of modern Christianity, which must constantly renew its self-understanding setting out from its roots. On this subject, all we can attempt here are a few brief observations. First we must ask ourselves: what does "progress" really mean; what does it promise and what does it not promise? In the nineteenth century, faith in progress was already subject to critique. In the twentieth century, Theodor W. Adorno formulated the problem of faith in progress quite drastically: he said that progress, seen accurately, is progress from the sling to the atom bomb. Now this is certainly an aspect of progress that must not be concealed. To put it another way: the ambiguity of progress becomes evident. Without doubt, it offers new possibilities for good, but it also opens up appalling possibilities for evil - possibilities that formerly did not exist. We have all witnessed the way in which progress, in the wrong hands, can become and has indeed become a terrifying progress in evil. If technical progress is not matched by corresponding progress in man's ethical formation, in man's inner growth (cf. *Ep* 3:16; 2 *Co* 4:16), then it is not progress at all, but a threat for man and for the world.

23. As far as the two great themes of "reason" and "freedom" are concerned, here we can only touch upon the issues connected with them. Yes indeed, reason is God's great gift to man, and the victory of reason over unreason is also a goal of the Christian life. But when does reason truly triumph? When it is detached from God? When it has become blind to God? Is the reason behind action and capacity for action the whole of reason? If progress, in order to be progress, needs moral growth on the part of humanity, then the reason behind action and capacity for action is likewise urgently in need of integration through reason's openness to the saving forces

76

of faith, to the differentiation between good and evil. Only thus does reason become truly human. It becomes human only if it is capable of directing the will along the right path, and it is capable of this only if it looks beyond itself. Otherwise, man's situation, in view of the imbalance between his material capacity and the lack of judgement in his heart, becomes a threat for him and for creation. Thus where freedom is concerned, we must remember that human freedom always requires a convergence of various freedoms. Yet this convergence cannot succeed unless it is determined by a common intrinsic criterion of measurement, which is the foundation and goal of our freedom. Let us put it very simply: man needs God, otherwise he remains without hope. Given the developments of the modern age, the quotation from Saint Paul with which I began (*Ep* 2:12) proves to be thoroughly realistic and plainly true. There is no doubt, therefore, that a "Kingdom of God" accomplished without God - a kingdom therefore of man alone - inevitably ends up as the "perverse end" of all things as described by Kant: we have seen it, and we see it over and over again. Yet neither is there any doubt that God truly enters into human affairs only when, rather than being present merely in our thinking, he himself comes towards us and speaks to us. Reason therefore needs faith if it is to be completely itself: reason and faith need one another in order to fulfil their true nature and their mission.

The true shape of Christian hope

24. Let us ask once again: what may we hope? And what may we not hope? First of all, we must acknowledge that incremental progress is possible only in the material sphere. Here, amid our growing knowledge of the structure of matter and in the light of ever more advanced inventions, we clearly see continuous progress towards an ever greater mastery of nature. Yet in the field of ethical awareness and moral decision-making, there is no similar possibility of accumulation for the simple reason that man's freedom is always new and he must always make his decisions anew. These decisions can never simply be made for us in advance by others - if that were

the case, we would no longer be free. Freedom presupposes that in fundamental decisions, every person and every generation is a new beginning. Naturally, new generations can build on the knowledge and experience of those who went before, and they can draw upon the moral treasury of the whole of humanity. But they can also reject it, because it can never be self-evident in the same way as material inventions. The moral treasury of humanity is not readily at hand like tools that we use; it is present as an appeal to freedom and a possibility for it. This, however, means that:

a) The right state of human affairs, the moral well-being of the world can never be guaranteed simply through structures alone, however good they are. Such structures are not only important, but necessary; yet they cannot and must not marginalise human freedom. Even the best structures function only when the community is animated by convictions capable of motivating people to assent freely to the social order. Freedom requires conviction; conviction does not exist on its own, but must always be gained anew by the community.

b) Since man always remains free and since his freedom is always fragile, the kingdom of good will never be definitively established in this world. Anyone who promises the better world that is guaranteed to last for ever is making a false promise; he is overlooking human freedom. Freedom must constantly be won over for the cause of good. Free assent to the good never exists simply by itself. If there were structures which could irrevocably guarantee a determined - good - state of the world, man's freedom would be denied, and hence they would not be good structures at all.

25. What this means is that every generation has the task of engaging anew in the arduous search for the right way to order human affairs; this task is never simply completed. Yet every generation must also make its own contribution to establishing convincing structures of freedom and of good, which can help the following generation as a guideline for the proper use of human freedom; hence, always within human limits, they provide a certain guarantee also for the future. In other words: good structures help, but of themselves they

are not enough. Man can never be redeemed simply from outside. Francis Bacon and those who followed in the intellectual current of modernity that he inspired were wrong to believe that man would be redeemed through science. Such an expectation asks too much of science; this kind of hope is deceptive. Science can contribute greatly to making the world and mankind more human. Yet it can also destroy mankind and the world unless it is steered by forces that lie outside it. On the other hand, we must also acknowledge that modern Christianity, faced with the successes of science in progressively structuring the world, has to a large extent restricted its attention to the individual and his salvation. In so doing it has limited the horizon of its hope and has failed to recognise sufficiently the greatness of its task - even if it has continued to achieve great things in the formation of man and in care for the weak and the suffering.

26. It is not science that redeems man: man is redeemed by love. This applies even in terms of this present world. When someone has the experience of a great love in his life, this is a moment of "redemption" which gives a new meaning to his life. But soon he will also realise that the love bestowed upon him cannot by itself resolve the question of his life. It is a love that remains fragile. It can be destroyed by death. The human being needs unconditional love. He needs the certainty which makes him say: "neither death, nor life, nor angels, nor principalities, nor things present, nor things to come, nor powers, nor height, nor depth, nor anything else in all creation, will be able to separate us from the love of God in Christ Jesus our Lord" (*Rm* 8:38-39). If this absolute love exists, with its absolute certainty, then - only then - is man "redeemed", whatever should happen to him in his particular circumstances. This is what it means to say: Jesus Christ has "redeemed" us. Through him we have become certain of God, a God who is not a remote "first cause" of the world, because his only-begotten Son has become man and of him everyone can say: "I live by faith in the Son of God, who loved me and gave himself for me" (*Ga* 2:20).

27. In this sense it is true that anyone who does not know God, even though he may entertain all kinds of hopes, is ultimately without hope, without the great hope that sustains the whole of life (cf. *Ep* 2:12). Man's great, true hope which holds firm in spite of all disappointments can only be God - God who has loved us and who continues to love us "to the end," until all "is accomplished" (cf. *Jn* 13:1 and 19:30). Whoever is moved by love begins to perceive what "life" really is. He begins to perceive the meaning of the word of hope that we encountered in the Baptismal Rite: from faith I await "eternal life" - the true life which, whole and unthreatened, in all its fullness, is simply life. Jesus, who said that he had come so that we might have life and have it in its fullness, in abundance (cf. *Jn* 10:10), has also explained to us what "life" means: "this is eternal life, that they know you the only true God, and Jesus Christ whom you have sent" (*Jn* 17:3). Life in its true sense is not something we have exclusively in or from ourselves: it is a relationship. And life in its totality is a relationship with him who is the source of life. If we are in relation with him who does not die, who is Life itself and Love itself, then we are in life. Then we "live".

28. Yet now the question arises: are we not in this way falling back once again into an individualistic understanding of salvation, into hope for myself alone, which is not true hope since it forgets and overlooks others? Indeed we are not! Our relationship with God is established through communion with Jesus - we cannot achieve it alone or from our own resources alone. The relationship with Jesus, however, is a relationship with the one who gave himself as a ransom for all (cf. 1 *Tm* 2:6). Being in communion with Jesus Christ draws us into his "being for all"; it makes it our own way of being. He commits us to live for others, but only through communion with him does it become possible truly to be there for others, for the whole. In this regard I would like to quote the great Greek Doctor of the Church, Maximus the Confessor (d. 662), who begins by exhorting us to prefer nothing to the knowledge and love of God, but then quickly moves on to practicalities: "The one who loves God cannot hold on to money but rather gives it out in

God's fashion...in the same manner in accordance with the measure of justice."[19] Love of God leads to participation in the justice and generosity of God towards others. Loving God requires an interior freedom from all possessions and all material goods: the love of God is revealed in responsibility for others.[20] This same connection between love of God and responsibility for others can be seen in a striking way in the life of Saint Augustine. After his conversion to the Christian faith, he decided, together with some like-minded friends, to lead a life totally dedicated to the word of God and to things eternal. His intention was to practise a Christian version of the ideal of the contemplative life expressed in the great tradition of Greek philosophy, choosing in this way the "better part" (cf. *Lk* 10:42). Things turned out differently, however. While attending the Sunday liturgy at the port city of Hippo, he was called out from the assembly by the Bishop and constrained to receive ordination for the exercise of the priestly ministry in that city. Looking back on that moment, he writes in his *Confessions*: "Terrified by my sins and the weight of my misery, I had resolved in my heart, and meditated flight into the wilderness; but you forbade me and gave me strength, by saying: 'Christ died for all, that those who live might live no longer for themselves but for him who for their sake died' (cf. 2 *Co* 5:15)".[21] Christ died for all. To live for him means allowing oneself to be drawn into his *being for others*.

29. For Augustine this meant a totally new life. He once described his daily life in the following terms: "The turbulent have to be corrected, the faint-hearted cheered up, the weak supported; the Gospel's opponents need to be refuted, its insidious enemies guarded against; the unlearned need to be taught, the indolent stirred up, the argumentative checked; the proud must be put in their place, the desperate set on their feet, those engaged in quarrels reconciled; the needy have to be helped, the oppressed to be liberated, the good

---

[19] *Chapters on charity, Centuria* 1, ch. 1: *PG* 90, 965.

[20] Cf. *ibid.*: *PG* 90, 962-966.

[21] *Conf.* X 43, 70: *CSEL* 33, 279.

to be encouraged, the bad to be tolerated; all must be loved."[22] "The Gospel terrifies me"[23] - producing that healthy fear which prevents us from living for ourselves alone and compels us to pass on the hope we hold in common. Amid the serious difficulties facing the Roman Empire - and also posing a serious threat to Roman Africa, which was actually destroyed at the end of Augustine's life - this was what he set out to do: to transmit hope, the hope which came to him from faith and which, in complete contrast with his introverted temperament, enabled him to take part decisively and with all his strength in the task of building up the city. In the same chapter of the *Confessions* in which we have just noted the decisive reason for his commitment "for all", he says that Christ "intercedes for us, otherwise I should despair. My weaknesses are many and grave, many and grave indeed, but more abundant still is your medicine. We might have thought that your word was far distant from union with man, and so we might have despaired of ourselves, if this Word had not become flesh and dwelt among us."[24] On the strength of his hope, Augustine dedicated himself completely to the ordinary people and to his city - renouncing his spiritual nobility, he preached and acted in a simple way for simple people.

30. Let us summarise what has emerged so far in the course of our reflections. Day by day, man experiences many greater or lesser hopes, different in kind according to the different periods of his life. Sometimes one of these hopes may appear to be totally satisfying without any need for other hopes. Young people can have the hope of a great and fully satisfying love; the hope of a certain position in their profession, or of some success that will prove decisive for the rest of their lives. When these hopes are fulfilled, however, it becomes clear that they were not, in reality, the whole. It becomes evident that man has need of a hope that goes further. It becomes clear that only something infinite will suffice for him, something that will always be more than he can ever attain. In this regard

[22] *Sermo* 340, 3: *PL* 38, 1484; cf. F. Van der Meer, *Augustine the Bishop*, London and New York 1961, p. 268.

[23] *Sermo* 339, 4: *PL* 38, 1481.

[24] *Conf.* X 43, 69: *CSEL* 33, 279.

our contemporary age has developed the hope of creating a perfect world that, thanks to scientific knowledge and to scientifically based politics, seemed to be achievable. Thus Biblical hope in the Kingdom of God has been displaced by hope in the kingdom of man, the hope of a better world which would be the real "Kingdom of God". This seemed at last to be the great and realistic hope that man needs. It was capable of galvanising - for a time - all man's energies. The great objective seemed worthy of full commitment. In the course of time, however, it has become clear that this hope is constantly receding. Above all it has become apparent that this may be a hope for a future generation, but not for me. And however much "for all" may be part of the great hope - since I cannot be happy without others or in opposition to them - it remains true that a hope that does not concern me personally is not a real hope. It has also become clear that this hope is opposed to freedom, since human affairs depend in each generation on the free decisions of those concerned. If this freedom were to be taken away, as a result of certain conditions or structures, then ultimately this world would not be good, since a world without freedom can by no means be a good world. Hence, while we must always be committed to the improvement of the world, tomorrow's better world cannot be the proper and sufficient content of our hope. And in this regard the question always arises: when is the world "better"? What makes it good? By what standard are we to judge its goodness? What are the paths that lead to this "goodness"?

31. Let us say once again: we need the greater and lesser hopes that keep us going day by day. But these are not enough without the great hope, which must surpass everything else. This great hope can only be God, who encompasses the whole of reality and who can bestow upon us what we, by ourselves, cannot attain. The fact that it comes to us as a gift is actually part of hope. God is the foundation of hope: not any god, but the God who has a human face and who has loved us to the end, each one of us and humanity in its entirety. His Kingdom is not an imaginary hereafter, situated in a future that will never arrive; his Kingdom is present wherever he is

loved and wherever his love reaches us. His love alone gives us the possibility of soberly persevering day by day, without ceasing to be spurred on by hope, in a world which by its very nature is imperfect. His love is at the same time our guarantee of the existence of what we only vaguely sense and which nevertheless, in our deepest self, we await: a life that is "truly" life. Let us now, in the final section, develop this idea in more detail as we focus our attention on some of the "settings" in which we can learn in practice about hope and its exercise.

"Settings" for learning and practising hope

I. Prayer as a school of hope

32. A first essential setting for learning hope is prayer. When no one listens to me any more, God still listens to me. When I can no longer talk to anyone or call upon anyone, I can always talk to God. When there is no longer anyone to help me deal with a need or expectation that goes beyond the human capacity for hope, he can help me.[25] When I have been plunged into complete solitude...; if I pray I am never totally alone. The late Cardinal Nguyen Van Thuan, a prisoner for thirteen years, nine of them spent in solitary confinement, has left us a precious little book: *Prayers of Hope*. During thirteen years in jail, in a situation of seemingly utter hopelessness, the fact that he could listen and speak to God became for him an increasing power of hope, which enabled him, after his release, to become for people all over the world a witness to hope - to that great hope which does not wane even in the nights of solitude.

33. Saint Augustine, in a homily on the *First Letter of John*, describes very beautifully the intimate relationship between prayer and hope. He defines prayer as an exercise of desire. Man was created for greatness - for God himself; he was created to be filled by God. But his heart is too small for the greatness to which it is destined. It must be stretched. "By delaying [his gift], God strengthens our desire; through desire he enlarges our soul and by expanding it he increases its capacity [for receiving him]". Augustine refers to Saint Paul, who speaks of himself as straining forward to the things that are to come (cf. *Ph* 3:13). He then uses a very beautiful image to describe this process of enlargement and preparation of the human heart. "Suppose that God wishes to fill you with honey [a symbol of God's tenderness and goodness]; but if you are full of vinegar, where will you put the honey?" The vessel, that is your heart, must first be enlarged and then cleansed, freed from the vinegar and its taste. This requires hard work and

---

[25] Cf. *Catechism of the Catholic Church*, 2657.

is painful, but in this way alone do we become suited to that for which we are destined.[26] Even if Augustine speaks directly only of our capacity for God, it is nevertheless clear that through this effort by which we are freed from vinegar and the taste of vinegar, not only are we made free for God, but we also become open to others. It is only by becoming children of God, that we can be with our common Father. To pray is not to step outside history and withdraw to our own private corner of happiness. When we pray properly we undergo a process of inner purification which opens us up to God and thus to our fellow human beings as well. In prayer we must learn what we can truly ask of God - what is worthy of God. We must learn that we cannot pray against others. We must learn that we cannot ask for the superficial and comfortable things that we desire at this moment - that meagre, misplaced hope that leads us away from God. We must learn to purify our desires and our hopes. We must free ourselves from the hidden lies with which we deceive ourselves. God sees through them, and when we come before God, we too are forced to recognise them. "But who can discern his errors? Clear me from hidden faults" prays the Psalmist (*Ps* 19:12 [18:13]). Failure to recognise my guilt, the illusion of my innocence, does not justify me and does not save me, because I am culpable for the numbness of my conscience and my incapacity to recognise the evil in me for what it is. If God does not exist, perhaps I have to seek refuge in these lies, because there is no one who can forgive me; no one who is the true criterion. Yet my encounter with God awakens my conscience in such a way that it no longer aims at self-justification, and is no longer a mere reflection of me and those of my contemporaries who shape my thinking, but it becomes a capacity for listening to the Good itself.

34. For prayer to develop this power of purification, it must on the one hand be something very personal, an encounter between my intimate self and God, the living God. On the other hand it must be constantly guided and enlightened by the great prayers of the Church and of the saints, by liturgical prayer, in which the Lord

---

[26] Cf. *In I Ioannis* 4, 6: *PL* 35, 2008f.

teaches us again and again how to pray properly. Cardinal Nguyen Van Thuan, in his book of spiritual exercises, tells us that during his life there were long periods when he was unable to pray and that he would hold fast to the texts of the Church's prayer: the Our Father, the Hail Mary and the prayers of the liturgy.[27] Praying must always involve this intermingling of public and personal prayer. This is how we can speak to God and how God speaks to us. In this way we undergo those purifications by which we become open to God and are prepared for the service of our fellow human beings. We become capable of the great hope, and thus we become ministers of hope for others. Hope in a Christian sense is always hope for others as well. It is an active hope, in which we struggle to prevent things moving towards the "perverse end". It is an active hope also in the sense that we keep the world open to God. Only in this way does it continue to be a truly human hope.

II. Action and suffering as settings for learning hope

35. All serious and upright human conduct is hope in action. This is so first of all in the sense that we thereby strive to realise our lesser and greater hopes, to complete this or that task which is important for our onward journey, or we work towards a brighter and more humane world so as to open doors into the future. Yet our daily efforts in pursuing our own lives and in working for the world's future either tire us or turn into fanaticism, unless we are enlightened by the radiance of the great hope that cannot be destroyed even by small-scale failures or by a breakdown in matters of historic importance. If we cannot hope for more than is effectively attainable at any given time, or more than is promised by political or economic authorities, our lives will soon be without hope. It is important to know that I can always continue to hope, even if in my own life, or the historical period in which I am living, there seems to be nothing left to hope for. Only the great certitude of hope that my own life and history in general, despite all failures, are held firm by the indestructible power of Love, and that this gives them their meaning and importance, only this kind of hope can then give

---

[27] *Testimony of Hope*, Boston 2000, pp. 121ff.

the courage to act and to persevere. Certainly we cannot "build" the Kingdom of God by our own efforts - what we build will always be the kingdom of man with all the limitations proper to our human nature. The Kingdom of God is a gift, and precisely because of this, it is great and beautiful, and constitutes the response to our hope. And we cannot - to use the classical expression - "merit" Heaven through our works. Heaven is always more than we could merit, just as being loved is never something "merited", but always a gift. However, even when we are fully aware that Heaven far exceeds what we can merit, it will always be true that our behaviour is not indifferent before God and therefore is not indifferent for the unfolding of history. We can open ourselves and the world and allow God to enter: we can open ourselves to truth, to love, to what is good. This is what the saints did, those who, as "God's fellow workers", contributed to the world's salvation (cf. 1 *Co* 3:9; 1 *Th* 3:2). We can free our life and the world from the poisons and contaminations that could destroy the present and the future. We can uncover the sources of creation and keep them unsullied, and in this way we can make a right use of creation, which comes to us as a gift, according to its intrinsic requirements and ultimate purpose. This makes sense even if outwardly we achieve nothing or seem powerless in the face of overwhelming hostile forces. So on the one hand, our actions engender hope for us and for others; but at the same time, it is the great hope based upon God's promises that gives us courage and directs our action in good times and bad.

36. Like action, suffering is a part of our human existence. Suffering stems partly from our finitude, and partly from the mass of sin which has accumulated over the course of history, and continues to grow unabated today. Certainly we must do whatever we can to reduce suffering: to avoid as far as possible the suffering of the innocent; to soothe pain; to give assistance in overcoming mental suffering. These are obligations both in justice and in love, and they are included among the fundamental requirements of the Christian life and every truly human life. Great progress has been made in the battle against physical pain; yet the sufferings of the innocent

and mental suffering have, if anything, increased in recent decades. Indeed, we must do all we can to overcome suffering, but to banish it from the world altogether is not in our power.

This is simply because we are unable to shake off our finitude and because none of us is capable of eliminating the power of evil, of sin which, as we plainly see, is a constant source of suffering. Only God is able to do this: only a God who personally enters history by making himself man and suffering within history. We know that this God exists, and hence that this power to "take away the sin of the world" (*Jn* 1:29) is present in the world. Through faith in the existence of this power, hope for the world's healing has emerged in history. It is, however, hope - not yet fulfilment; hope that gives us the courage to place ourselves on the side of good even in seemingly hopeless situations, aware that, as far as the external course of history is concerned, the power of sin will continue to be a terrible presence.

37. Let us return to our topic. We can try to limit suffering, to fight against it, but we cannot eliminate it. It is when we attempt to avoid suffering by withdrawing from anything that might involve hurt, when we try to spare ourselves the effort and pain of pursuing truth, love, and goodness, that we drift into a life of emptiness, in which there may be almost no pain, but the dark sensation of meaninglessness and abandonment is all the greater. It is not by sidestepping or fleeing from suffering that we are healed, but rather by our capacity for accepting it, maturing through it and finding meaning through union with Christ, who suffered with infinite love. In this context, I would like to quote a passage from a letter written by the Vietnamese martyr Paul Le-Bao-Tinh (d. 1857) which illustrates this transformation of suffering through the power of hope springing from faith. "I, Paul, in chains for the name of Christ, wish to relate to you the trials besetting me daily, in order that you may be inflamed with love for God and join with me in his praises, for his mercy is for ever (*Ps* 136 [135]). The prison here is a true image of everlasting Hell: to cruel tortures of every kind - shackles, iron chains, manacles - are added hatred, vengeance,

Spe Salvi

calumnies, obscene speech, quarrels, evil acts, swearing, curses, as well as anguish and grief. But the God who once freed the three children from the fiery furnace is with me always; he has delivered me from these tribulations and made them sweet, for his mercy is for ever. In the midst of these torments, which usually terrify others, I am, by the grace of God, full of joy and gladness, because I am not alone - Christ is with me... How am I to bear with the spectacle, as each day I see emperors, mandarins, and their retinue blaspheming your holy name, O Lord, who are enthroned above the Cherubim and Seraphim? (cf. *Ps* 80:1 [79:2]). Behold, the pagans have trodden your Cross underfoot! Where is your glory? As I see all this, I would, in the ardent love I have for you, prefer to be torn limb from limb and to die as a witness to your love. O Lord, show your power, save me, sustain me, that in my infirmity your power may be shown and may be glorified before the nations... Beloved brothers, as you hear all these things may you give endless thanks in joy to God, from whom every good proceeds; bless the Lord with me, for his mercy is for ever...I write these things to you in order that your faith and mine may be united. In the midst of this storm I cast my anchor towards the throne of God, the anchor that is the lively hope in my heart."[28] This is a letter from "Hell". It lays bare all the horror of a concentration camp, where to the torments inflicted by tyrants upon their victims is added the outbreak of evil in the victims themselves, such that they in turn become further instruments of their persecutors' cruelty. This is indeed a letter from Hell, but it also reveals the truth of the Psalm text: "If I go up to the heavens, you are there; if I sink to the nether world, you are present there... If I say, 'Surely the darkness shall hide me, and night shall be my light' - for you darkness itself is not dark, and night shines as the day; darkness and light are the same" (*Ps* 139 [138]:8-12; cf. also *Ps* 23 [22]:4). Christ descended into "Hell" and is therefore close to those cast into it, transforming their darkness into light. Suffering and torment is still terrible and well-nigh unbearable. Yet the star of hope has risen - the anchor of the heart reaches the very throne of God. Instead of evil being unleashed within man, the

---

[28] The Liturgy of the Hours, Office of Readings, 24th November.

90

light shines victorious: suffering - without ceasing to be suffering - becomes, despite everything, a hymn of praise.

38. The true measure of humanity is essentially determined in relationship to suffering and to the sufferer. This holds true both for the individual and for society. A society unable to accept its suffering members and incapable of helping to share their suffering and to bear it inwardly through "com-passion" is a cruel and inhuman society. Yet society cannot accept its suffering members and support them in their trials unless individuals are capable of doing so themselves; moreover, the individual cannot accept another's suffering unless he personally is able to find meaning in suffering, a path of purification and growth in maturity, a journey of hope. Indeed, to accept the "other" who suffers, means that I take up his suffering in such a way that it becomes mine also. Because it has now become a shared suffering, though, in which another person is present, this suffering is penetrated by the light of love. The Latin word *con-solatio,* "consolation", expresses this beautifully. It suggests *being with* the other in his solitude, so that it ceases to be solitude. Furthermore, the capacity to accept suffering for the sake of goodness, truth and justice is an essential criterion of humanity, because if my own well-being and safety are ultimately more important than truth and justice, then the power of the stronger prevails, then violence and untruth reign supreme. Truth and justice must stand above my comfort and physical well-being, or else my life itself becomes a lie. In the end, even the "yes" to love is a source of suffering, because love always requires expropriations of my "I", in which I allow myself to be pruned and wounded. Love simply cannot exist without this painful renunciation of myself, for otherwise it becomes pure selfishness and thereby ceases to be love.

39. To suffer with the other and for others; to suffer for the sake of truth and justice; to suffer out of love and in order to become a person who truly loves - these are fundamental elements of humanity, and to abandon them would destroy man himself. Yet once again the question arises: are we capable of this? Is the other

important enough to warrant my becoming, on his account, a person who suffers? Does truth matter to me enough to make suffering worthwhile? Is the promise of love so great that it justifies the gift of myself? In the history of humanity, it was the Christian faith that had the particular merit of bringing forth within man a new and deeper capacity for these kinds of suffering that are decisive for his humanity. The Christian faith has shown us that truth, justice and love are not simply ideals, but enormously weighty realities. It has shown us that God - Truth and Love in person - desired to suffer for us and with us. Bernard of Clairvaux coined the marvellous expression: *Impassibilis est Deus, sed non incompassibilis*[29] - God cannot suffer, but he can *suffer with*. Man is worth so much to God that he himself became man in order to *suffer with* man in an utterly real way - in flesh and blood - as is revealed to us in the account of Jesus's Passion. Hence in all human suffering we are joined by one who experiences and carries that suffering *with* us; hence *con-solatio* is present in all suffering, the consolation of God's compassionate love - and so the star of hope rises. Certainly, in our many different sufferings and trials we always need the lesser and greater hopes too - a kind visit, the healing of internal and external wounds, a favourable resolution of a crisis, and so on. In our lesser trials these kinds of hope may even be sufficient. But in truly great trials, where I must make a definitive decision to place the truth before my own welfare, career and possessions, I need the certitude of that true, great hope of which we have spoken here. For this too we need witnesses - martyrs - who have given themselves totally, so as to show us the way - day after day. We need them if we are to prefer goodness to comfort, even in the little choices we face each day - knowing that this is how we live life to the full. Let us say it once again: the capacity to suffer for the sake of the truth is the measure of humanity. Yet this capacity to suffer depends on the type and extent of the hope that we bear within us and build upon. The saints were able to make the great journey of human existence in the way that Christ had done before them, because they were brimming with great hope.

---

[29] *Sermones in Cant., Sermo* 26, 5: *PL* 183, 906.

40. I would like to add here another brief comment with some relevance for everyday living. There used to be a form of devotion - perhaps less practised today but quite widespread not long ago - that included the idea of "offering up" the minor daily hardships that continually strike at us like irritating "jabs", thereby giving them a meaning. Of course, there were some exaggerations and perhaps unhealthy applications of this devotion, but we need to ask ourselves whether there may not after all have been something essential and helpful contained within it. What does it mean to offer something up? Those who did so were convinced that they could insert these little annoyances into Christ's great "com-passion" so that they somehow became part of the treasury of compassion so greatly needed by the human race. In this way, even the small inconveniences of daily life could acquire meaning and contribute to the economy of good and of human love. Maybe we should consider whether it might be judicious to revive this practice ourselves.

III. Judgement as a setting for learning and practising hope

41. At the conclusion of the central section of the Church's great *Credo* - the part that recounts the mystery of Christ, from his eternal birth of the Father and his temporal birth of the Virgin Mary, through his Cross and Resurrection to the second coming - we find the phrase: "he will come again in glory to judge the living and the dead". From the earliest times, the prospect of the Judgement has influenced Christians in their daily living as a criterion by which to order their present life, as a summons to their conscience, and at the same time as hope in God's justice. Faith in Christ has never looked merely backwards or merely upwards, but always also forwards to the hour of justice that the Lord repeatedly proclaimed. This looking ahead has given Christianity its importance for the present moment. In the arrangement of Christian sacred buildings, which were intended to make visible the historic and cosmic breadth of faith in Christ, it became customary to depict the Lord returning as a king - the symbol of hope - at the east end; while the west wall normally portrayed the Last Judgement as a symbol

of our responsibility for our lives - a scene which followed and accompanied the faithful as they went out to resume their daily routine. As the iconography of the Last Judgement developed, however, more and more prominence was given to its ominous and frightening aspects, which obviously held more fascination for artists than the splendour of hope, often all too well concealed beneath the horrors.

42. In the modern era, the idea of the Last Judgement has faded into the background: Christian faith has been individualised and primarily oriented towards the salvation of the believer's own soul, while reflection on world history is largely dominated by the idea of progress. The fundamental content of awaiting a final Judgement, however, has not disappeared: it has simply taken on a totally different form. The atheism of the nineteenth and twentieth centuries is - in its origins and aims - a type of moralism: a protest against the injustices of the world and of world history. A world marked by so much injustice, innocent suffering, and cynicism of power cannot be the work of a good God. A God with responsibility for such a world would not be a just God, much less a good God. It is for the sake of morality that this God has to be contested. Since there is no God to create justice, it seems man himself is now called to establish justice. If in the face of this world's suffering, protest against God is understandable, the claim that humanity can and must do what no God actually does or is able to do is both presumptuous and intrinsically false. It is no accident that this idea has led to the greatest forms of cruelty and violations of justice; rather, it is grounded in the intrinsic falsity of the claim. A world which has to create its own justice is a world without hope. No one and nothing can answer for centuries of suffering. No one and nothing can guarantee that the cynicism of power - whatever beguiling ideological mask it adopts - will cease to dominate the world. This is why the great thinkers of the Frankfurt School, Max Horkheimer and Theodor W. Adorno, were equally critical of atheism and theism. Horkheimer radically excluded the possibility of ever finding a this-worldly substitute for God, while at the same

time he rejected the image of a good and just God. In an extreme radicalisation of the Old Testament prohibition of images, he speaks of a "longing for the totally Other" that remains inaccessible - a cry of yearning directed at world history. Adorno also firmly upheld this total rejection of images, which naturally meant the exclusion of any "image" of a loving God. On the other hand, he also constantly emphasised this "negative" dialectic and asserted that justice - true justice - would require a world "where not only present suffering would be wiped out, but also that which is irrevocably past would be undone."[30] This, would mean, however - to express it with positive and hence, for him, inadequate symbols - that there can be no justice without a resurrection of the dead. Yet this would have to involve "the resurrection of the flesh, something that is totally foreign to idealism and the realm of Absolute spirit."[31]

43. Christians likewise can and must constantly learn from the strict rejection of images that is contained in God's first commandment (cf. *Ex* 20:4). The truth of negative theology was highlighted by the Fourth Lateran Council, which explicitly stated that however great the similarity that may be established between Creator and creature, the dissimilarity between them is always greater.[32] In any case, for the believer the rejection of images cannot be carried so far that one ends up, as Horkheimer and Adorno would like, by saying "no" to both theses - theism and atheism. God has given himself an "image": in Christ who was made man. In him who was crucified, the denial of false images of God is taken to an extreme. God now reveals his true face in the figure of the sufferer who shares man's Godforsaken condition by taking it upon himself. This innocent sufferer has attained the certitude of hope: there is a God, and God can create justice in a way that we cannot conceive, yet we can begin to grasp it through faith. Yes, there is a resurrection of the

[30] *Negative Dialektik* (1966), Third part, III, 11, in *Gesammelte Schriften* VI, Frankfurt am Main 1973, p. 395.

[31] *Ibid.,* Second part, p. 207.

[32] DS 806.

flesh.[33] There is justice.[34] There is an "undoing" of past suffering, a reparation that sets things aright. For this reason, faith in the Last Judgement is first and foremost hope - the need for which was made abundantly clear in the upheavals of recent centuries. I am convinced that the question of justice constitutes the essential argument, or in any case the strongest argument, in favour of faith in eternal life. The purely individual need for a fulfilment that is denied to us in this life, for an everlasting love that we await, is certainly an important motive for believing that man was made for eternity; but only in connection with the impossibility that the injustice of history should be the final word does the necessity for Christ's return and for new life become fully convincing.

44. To protest against God in the name of justice is not helpful. A world without God is a world without hope (cf. *Ep* 2:12). Only God can create justice. And faith gives us the certainty that he does so. The image of the Last Judgement is not primarily an image of terror, but an image of hope; for us it may even be the decisive image of hope. Is it not also a frightening image? I would say: it is an image that evokes responsibility, an image, therefore, of that fear of which Saint Hilary spoke when he said that all our fear has its place in love.[35] God is justice and creates justice. This is our consolation and our hope. And in his justice there is also grace. This we know by turning our gaze to the crucified and risen Christ. Both these things - justice and grace - must be seen in their correct inner relationship. Grace does not cancel out justice. It does not make wrong into right. It is not a sponge which wipes everything away, so that whatever someone has done on earth ends up being of equal value. Dostoevsky, for example, was right to protest against this kind of Heaven and this kind of grace in his novel *The Brothers Karamazov*. Evildoers, in the end, do not sit at table at the eternal banquet beside their victims without distinction, as though nothing had happened. Here I would like to quote a passage from Plato

---

[33] Cf. *Catechism of the Catholic Church*, 988-1004.

[34] Cf. *ibid.*, 1040.

[35] Cf. *Tractatus super Psalmos, Ps* 127, 1-3: *CSEL* 22, 628-630.

which expresses a premonition of just judgement that in many respects remains true and salutary for Christians too. Albeit using mythological images, he expresses the truth with an unambiguous clarity, saying that in the end souls will stand naked before the judge. It no longer matters what they once were in history, but only what they are in truth: "Often, when it is the king or some other monarch or potentate that he (the judge) has to deal with, he finds that there is no soundness in the soul whatever; he finds it scourged and scarred by the various acts of perjury and wrong-doing...it is twisted and warped by lies and vanity, and nothing is straight because truth has had no part in its development. Power, luxury, pride, and debauchery have left it so full of disproportion and ugliness that when he has inspected it (he) sends it straight to prison, where on its arrival it will undergo the appropriate punishment... Sometimes, though, the eye of the judge lights on a different soul which has lived in purity and truth...then he is struck with admiration and sends him to the isles of the blessed."[36] In the parable of the rich man and Lazarus (cf. *Lk* 16:19-31), Jesus admonishes us through the image of a soul destroyed by arrogance and opulence, who has created an impassable chasm between himself and the poor man; the chasm of being trapped within material pleasures; the chasm of forgetting the other, of incapacity to love, which then becomes a burning and unquenchable thirst. We must note that in this parable Jesus is not referring to the final destiny after the Last Judgement, but is taking up a notion found, *inter alia*, in early Judaism, namely that of an intermediate state between death and resurrection, a state in which the final sentence is yet to be pronounced.

45. This early Jewish idea of an intermediate state includes the view that these souls are not simply in a sort of temporary custody but, as the parable of the rich man illustrates, are already being punished or are experiencing a provisional form of bliss. There is also the idea that this state can involve purification and healing which mature the soul for communion with God. The early Church took up these concepts, and in the Western Church they gradually developed into the doctrine of Purgatory. We do not need to

---

[36] *Gorgias*, 525a-526c.

examine here the complex historical paths of this development; it is enough to ask what it actually means. With death, our life-choice becomes definitive - our life stands before the judge. Our choice, which in the course of an entire life takes on a certain shape, can have a variety of forms. There can be people who have totally destroyed their desire for truth and readiness to love, people for whom everything has become a lie, people who have lived for hatred and have suppressed all love within themselves. This is a terrifying thought, but alarming profiles of this type can be seen in certain figures of our own history. In such people all would be beyond remedy and the destruction of good would be irrevocable: this is what we mean by the word *Hell*.[37] On the other hand there can be people who are utterly pure, completely permeated by God, and thus fully open to their neighbours - people for whom communion with God even now gives direction to their entire being and whose journey towards God only brings to fulfilment what they already are.[38]

46. Yet we know from experience that neither case is normal in human life. For the great majority of people - we may suppose - there remains in the depths of their being an ultimate interior openness to truth, to love, to God. In the concrete choices of life, however, it is covered over by ever new compromises with evil - much filth covers purity, but the thirst for purity remains and it still constantly re-emerges from all that is base and remains present in the soul. What happens to such individuals when they appear before the Judge? Will all the impurity they have amassed through life suddenly cease to matter? What else might occur? Saint Paul, in his *First Letter to the Corinthians*, gives us an idea of the differing impact of God's judgement according to each person's particular circumstances. He does this using images which in some way try to express the invisible, without it being possible for us to conceptualise these images - simply because we can neither see into the world beyond death nor do we have

---

[37] Cf. *Catechism of the Catholic Church*, 1033-1037.

[38] Cf. *ibid.*, 1023-1029.

any experience of it. Paul begins by saying that Christian life is built upon a common foundation: Jesus Christ. This foundation endures. If we have stood firm on this foundation and built our life upon it, we know that it cannot be taken away from us even in death. Then Paul continues: "Now if any one builds on the foundation with gold, silver, precious stones, wood, hay, straw - each man's work will become manifest; for the Day will disclose it, because it will be revealed with fire, and the fire will test what sort of work each one has done. If the work which any man has built on the foundation survives, he will receive a reward. If any man's work is burned up, he will suffer loss, though he himself will be saved, but only as through fire" (1 *Co* 3:12-15). In this text, it is in any case evident that our salvation can take different forms, that some of what is built may be burned down, that in order to be saved we personally have to pass through "fire" so as to become fully open to receiving God and able to take our place at the table of the eternal marriage-feast.

47. Some recent theologians are of the opinion that the fire which both burns and saves is Christ himself, the Judge and Saviour. The encounter with him is the decisive act of judgement. Before his gaze all falsehood melts away. This encounter with him, as it burns us, transforms and frees us, allowing us to become truly ourselves. All that we build during our lives can prove to be mere straw, pure bluster, and it collapses. Yet in the pain of this encounter, when the impurity and sickness of our lives become evident to us, there lies salvation. His gaze, the touch of his heart heals us through an undeniably painful transformation "as through fire". But it is a blessed pain, in which the holy power of his love sears through us like a flame, enabling us to become totally ourselves and thus totally of God. In this way the inter-relation between justice and grace also becomes clear: the way we live our lives is not immaterial, but our defilement does not stain us for ever if we have at least continued to reach out towards Christ, towards truth and towards love. Indeed, it has already been burned away through Christ's Passion. At the moment of judgement we experience and

we absorb the overwhelming power of his love over all the evil in the world and in ourselves. The pain of love becomes our salvation and our joy. It is clear that we cannot calculate the "duration" of this transforming burning in terms of the chronological measurements of this world. The transforming "moment" of this encounter eludes earthly time-reckoning - it is the heart's time, it is the time of "passage" to communion with God in the Body of Christ.[39] The judgement of God is hope, both because it is justice and because it is grace. If it were merely grace, making all earthly things cease to matter, God would still owe us an answer to the question about justice - the crucial question that we ask of history and of God. If it were merely justice, in the end it could bring only fear to us all. The incarnation of God in Christ has so closely linked the two together - judgement and grace - that justice is firmly established: we all work out our salvation "with fear and trembling" (*Ph* 2:12). Nevertheless grace allows us all to hope, and to go trustfully to meet the Judge whom we know as our "advocate", or *parakletos* (cf. 1 *Jn* 2:1).

48. A further point must be mentioned here, because it is important for the practice of Christian hope. Early Jewish thought includes the idea that one can help the deceased in their intermediate state through prayer (see for example 2 *M* 12:38-45; first century BC). The equivalent practice was readily adopted by Christians and is common to the Eastern and Western Church. The East does not recognise the purifying and expiatory suffering of souls in the afterlife, but it does acknowledge various levels of beatitude and of suffering in the intermediate state. The souls of the departed can, however, receive "solace and refreshment" through the Eucharist, prayer and almsgiving. The belief that love can reach into the afterlife, that reciprocal giving and receiving is possible, in which our affection for one another continues beyond the limits of death - this has been a fundamental conviction of Christianity throughout the ages and it remains a source of comfort today. Who would not feel the need to convey to their departed loved ones

---

[39] Cf. *Catechism of the Catholic Church*, 1030-1032.

a sign of kindness, a gesture of gratitude or even a request for pardon? Now a further question arises: if "Purgatory" is simply purification through fire in the encounter with the Lord, Judge and Saviour, how can a third person intervene, even if he or she is particularly close to the other? When we ask such a question, we should recall that no man is an island, entire of itself. Our lives are involved with one another, through innumerable interactions they are linked together. No one lives alone. No one sins alone. No one is saved alone. The lives of others continually spill over into mine: in what I think, say, do and achieve. And conversely, my life spills over into that of others: for better and for worse. So my prayer for another is not something extraneous to that person, something external, not even after death. In the interconnectedness of Being, my gratitude to the other - my prayer for him - can play a small part in his purification. And for that there is no need to convert earthly time into God's time: in the communion of souls simple terrestrial time is superseded. It is never too late to touch the heart of another, nor is it ever in vain. In this way we further clarify an important element of the Christian concept of hope. Our hope is always essentially also hope for others; only thus is it truly hope for me too.[40] As Christians we should never limit ourselves to asking: how can I save myself? We should also ask: what can I do in order that others may be saved and that for them too the star of hope may rise? Then I will have done my utmost for my own personal salvation as well.

Mary, Star of Hope

49. With a hymn composed in the eighth or ninth century, thus for over a thousand years, the Church has greeted Mary, the Mother of God, as "Star of the Sea": *Ave maris stella*. Human life is a journey. Towards what destination? How do we find the way? Life is like a voyage on the sea of history, often dark and stormy, a voyage in which we watch for the stars that indicate the route. The true stars of our life are the people who have lived good lives. They are lights of

---

[40] Cf. *Catechism of the Catholic Church*, 1032.

hope. Certainly, Jesus Christ is the true light, the sun that has risen above all the shadows of history. But to reach him we also need lights close by - people who shine with his light and so guide us along our way. Who more than Mary could be a star of hope for us? With her "yes" she opened the door of our world to God himself; she became the living Ark of the Covenant, in whom God took flesh, became one of us, and pitched his tent among us (cf. *Jn* 1:14).

50. So we cry to her: Holy Mary, you belonged to the humble and great souls of Israel who, like Simeon, were "looking for the consolation of Israel" (*Lk* 2:25) and hoping, like Anna, "for the redemption of Jerusalem" (*Lk* 2:38). Your life was thoroughly imbued with the sacred scriptures of Israel which spoke of hope, of the promise made to Abraham and his descendants (cf. *Lk* 1:55). In this way we can appreciate the holy fear that overcame you when the angel of the Lord appeared to you and told you that you would give birth to the One who was the hope of Israel, the One awaited by the world. Through you, through your "yes", the hope of the ages became reality, entering this world and its history. You bowed low before the greatness of this task and gave your consent: "Behold, I am the handmaid of the Lord; let it be to me according to your word" (*Lk* 1:38). When you hastened with holy joy across the mountains of Judea to see your cousin Elizabeth, you became the image of the Church to come, which carries the hope of the world in her womb across the mountains of history. But alongside the joy which, with your *Magnificat,* you proclaimed in word and song for all the centuries to hear, you also knew the dark sayings of the prophets about the suffering of the servant of God in this world. Shining over his birth in the stable at Bethlehem, there were angels in splendour who brought the good news to the shepherds, but at the same time the lowliness of God in this world was all too palpable. The old man Simeon spoke to you of the sword which would pierce your soul (cf. *Lk* 2:35), of the sign of contradiction that your Son would be in this world. Then, when Jesus began his public ministry, you had to step aside, so that a new family could grow, the family which it was his mission to establish and which

would be made up of those who heard his word and kept it (cf. *Lk* 11:27). Notwithstanding the great joy that marked the beginning of Jesus's ministry, in the synagogue of Nazareth you must already have experienced the truth of the saying about the "sign of contradiction" (cf. *Lk* 4:28). In this way you saw the growing power of hostility and rejection which built up around Jesus until the hour of the Cross, when you had to look upon the Saviour of the world, the heir of David, the Son of God dying like a failure, exposed to mockery, between criminals. Then you received the word of Jesus: "Woman, behold, your Son!" (*Jn* 19:26). From the Cross you received a new mission. From the Cross you became a mother in a new way: the mother of all those who believe in your Son Jesus and wish to follow him. The sword of sorrow pierced your heart. Did hope die? Did the world remain definitively without light, and life without purpose? At that moment, deep down, you probably listened again to the word spoken by the angel in answer to your fear at the time of the Annunciation: "Do not be afraid, Mary!" (*Lk* 1:30). How many times had the Lord, your Son, said the same thing to his disciples: do not be afraid! In your heart, you heard this word again during the night of Golgotha. Before the hour of his betrayal he had said to his disciples: "Be of good cheer, I have overcome the world" (*Jn* 16:33). "Let not your hearts be troubled, neither let them be afraid" (*Jn* 14:27). "Do not be afraid, Mary!" In that hour at Nazareth the angel had also said to you: "Of his kingdom there will be no end" (*Lk* 1:33). Could it have ended before it began? No, at the foot of the Cross, on the strength of Jesus's own word, you became the mother of believers.

In this faith, which even in the darkness of Holy Saturday bore the certitude of hope, you made your way towards Easter morning. The joy of the Resurrection touched your heart and united you in a new way to the disciples, destined to become the family of Jesus through faith. In this way you were in the midst of the community of believers, who in the days following the Ascension prayed with one voice for the gift of the Holy Spirit (cf. *Ac* 1:14) and then received that gift on the day of Pentecost. The "Kingdom" of Jesus was not as might have been imagined. It began in that hour, and of this "Kingdom" there will be no end. Thus you remain in the midst of the disciples as their Mother, as the Mother of hope. Holy Mary, Mother of God, our Mother, teach us to believe, to hope, to love with you. Show us the way to his Kingdom! Star of the Sea, shine upon us and guide us on our way!

Given in Rome, at Saint Peter's, on 30th November, the Feast of Saint Andrew the Apostle, in the year 2007, the third of my Pontificate.

BENEDICT PP. XVI

ENCYCLICAL LETTER

CARITAS IN VERITATE

OF THE SUPREME PONTIFF

POPE BENEDICT XVI

TO THE BISHOPS, PRIESTS AND DEACONS
MEN AND WOMEN RELIGIOUS, THE LAY FAITHFUL
AND ALL PEOPLE OF GOOD WILL

ON INTEGRAL HUMAN DEVELOPMENT
IN CHARITY AND TRUTH

CONTENTS

INTRODUCTION

1. Charity in truth, to which Jesus Christ bore witness by his earthly life and especially by his death and resurrection, is the principal driving force behind the authentic development of every person and of all humanity. Love - *caritas* - is an extraordinary force which leads people to opt for courageous and generous engagement in the field of justice and peace. It is a force that has its origin in God, Eternal Love and Absolute Truth. Each person finds his good by adherence to God's plan for him, in order to realise it fully: in this plan, he finds his truth, and through adherence to this truth he becomes free (cf. *Jn* 8:22). To defend the truth, to articulate it with humility and conviction, and to bear witness to it in life are therefore exacting and indispensable forms of charity. Charity, in fact, "rejoices in the truth" (1 *Co* 13:6). All people feel the interior impulse to love authentically: love and truth never abandon them completely, because these are the vocation planted by God in the heart and mind of every human person. The search for love and truth is purified and liberated by Jesus Christ from the impoverishment that our humanity brings to it, and he reveals to us in all its fullness the initiative of love and the plan for true life that God has prepared for us. In Christ, charity in truth becomes the Face of his Person, a vocation for us to love our brothers and sisters in the truth of his plan. Indeed, he himself is the Truth (cf. *Jn* 14:6).

2. Charity is at the heart of the Church's social doctrine. Every responsibility and every commitment spelt out by that doctrine is derived from charity which, according to the teaching of Jesus, is the synthesis of the entire Law (cf. *Mt* 22:36-40). It gives real substance to the personal relationship with God and with neighbour; it is the principle not only of micro-relationships (with friends, with family members or within small groups) but also of macro-relationships (social, economic and political ones). For the Church, instructed by the Gospel, charity is everything because, as Saint John teaches (cf. 1 *Jn* 4:8,16) and as I recalled in my first Encyclical Letter, "God is

love" (*Deus Caritas Est*): everything has its origin in God's love, everything is shaped by it, everything is directed towards it. Love is God's greatest gift to humanity, it is his promise and our hope.

I am aware of the ways in which charity has been and continues to be misconstrued and emptied of meaning, with the consequent risk of being misinterpreted, detached from ethical living and, in any event, undervalued. In the social, juridical, cultural, political and economic fields - the contexts, in other words, that are most exposed to this danger - it is easily dismissed as irrelevant for interpreting and giving direction to moral responsibility. Hence the need to link charity with truth not only in the sequence, pointed out by Saint Paul, of *veritas in caritate* (*Ep* 4:15), but also in the inverse and complementary sequence of *caritas in veritate*. Truth needs to be sought, found and expressed within the "economy" of charity, but charity in its turn needs to be understood, confirmed and practised in the light of truth. In this way, not only do we do a service to charity enlightened by truth, but we also help give credibility to truth, demonstrating its persuasive and authenticating power in the practical setting of social living. This is a matter of no small account today, in a social and cultural context which relativises truth, often paying little heed to it and showing increasing reluctance to acknowledge its existence.

3. Through this close link with truth, charity can be recognised as an authentic expression of humanity and as an element of fundamental importance in human relations, including those of a public nature. *Only in truth does charity shine forth*, only in truth can charity be authentically lived. Truth is the light that gives meaning and value to charity. That light is both the light of reason and the light of faith, through which the intellect attains to the natural and supernatural truth of charity: it grasps its meaning as gift, acceptance, and communion. Without truth, charity degenerates into sentimentality. Love becomes an empty shell, to be filled in an arbitrary way. In a culture without truth, this is the fatal risk facing love. It falls prey to contingent subjective emotions and opinions, the word "love" is abused and distorted, to the point where it comes

to mean the opposite. Truth frees charity from the constraints of an emotionalism that deprives it of relational and social content, and of a fideism that deprives it of human and universal breathing-space. In the truth, charity reflects the personal yet public dimension of faith in the God of the Bible, who is both *Agápe* and *Lógos*: Charity and Truth, Love and Word.

4. Because it is filled with truth, charity can be understood in the abundance of its values, it can be shared and communicated. *Truth*, in fact, is *lógos* which creates *diá-logos*, and hence communication and communion. Truth, by enabling men and women to let go of their subjective opinions and impressions, allows them to move beyond cultural and historical limitations and to come together in the assessment of the value and substance of things. Truth opens and unites our minds in the *lógos* of love: this is the Christian proclamation and testimony of charity. In the present social and cultural context, where there is a widespread tendency to relativise truth, practising charity in truth helps people to understand that adhering to the values of Christianity is not merely useful but essential for building a good society and for true integral human development. A Christianity of charity without truth would be more or less interchangeable with a pool of good sentiments, helpful for social cohesion, but of little relevance. In other words, there would no longer be any real place for God in the world. Without truth, charity is confined to a narrow field devoid of relations. It is excluded from the plans and processes of promoting human development of universal range, in dialogue between knowledge and praxis.

5. Charity is love received and given. It is "grace" (*cháris*). Its source is the wellspring of the Father's love for the Son, in the Holy Spirit. Love comes down to us from the Son. It is creative love, through which we have our being; it is redemptive love, through which we are recreated. Love is revealed and made present by Christ (cf. *Jn* 13:1) and "poured into our hearts through the Holy Spirit" (*Rm* 5:5). As the objects of God's love, men and women

become subjects of charity, they are called to make themselves instruments of grace, so as to pour forth God's charity and to weave networks of charity.

This dynamic of charity received and given is what gives rise to the Church's social teaching, which is *caritas in veritate in re sociali*: the proclamation of the truth of Christ's love in society. This doctrine is a service to charity, but its locus is truth. Truth preserves and expresses charity's power to liberate in the ever-changing events of history. It is at the same time the truth of faith and of reason, both in the distinction and also in the convergence of those two cognitive fields. Development, social well-being, the search for a satisfactory solution to the grave socio-economic problems besetting humanity, all need this truth. What they need even more is that this truth should be loved and demonstrated. Without truth, without trust and love for what is true, there is no social conscience and responsibility, and social action ends up serving private interests and the logic of power, resulting in social fragmentation, especially in a globalised society at difficult times like the present.

6. "*Caritas in veritate*" is the principle around which the Church's social doctrine turns, a principle that takes on practical form in the criteria that govern moral action. I would like to consider two of these in particular, of special relevance to the commitment to development in an increasingly globalised society: *justice and the common good.*

First of all, justice. *Ubi societas, ibi ius*: every society draws up its own system of justice. *Charity goes beyond justice*, because to love is to give, to offer what is "mine" to the other; but it never lacks justice, which prompts us to give the other what is "his", what is due to him by reason of his being or his acting. I cannot "give" what is mine to the other, without first giving him what pertains

Introduction

to him in justice. If we love others with charity, then first of all we are just towards them. Not only is justice not extraneous to charity, not only is it not an alternative or parallel path to charity: justice is inseparable from charity,[1] and intrinsic to it. Justice is the primary way of charity or, in Paul VI's words, "the minimum measure" of it,[2] an integral part of the love "in deed and in truth" (1 *Jn* 3:18), to which Saint John exhorts us. On the one hand, charity demands justice: recognition and respect for the legitimate rights of individuals and peoples. It strives to build the *earthly city* according to law and justice. On the other hand, charity transcends justice and completes it in the logic of giving and forgiving.[3] The *earthly city* is promoted not merely by relationships of rights and duties, but to an even greater and more fundamental extent by relationships of gratuitousness, mercy and communion. Charity always manifests God's love in human relationships as well, it gives theological and salvific value to all commitment for justice in the world.

7. Another important consideration is the common good. To love someone is to desire that person's good and to take effective steps to secure it. Besides the good of the individual, there is a good that is linked to living in society: the common good. It is the good of "all of us", made up of individuals, families and intermediate groups who together constitute society.[4] It is a good that is sought not for its own sake, but for the people who belong to the social community and who can only really and effectively pursue their good within it. To desire the *common good* and strive towards it *is a requirement of justice and charity*. To take a stand for the common good is on the one hand to be solicitous for, and on the other hand to avail oneself of, that complex of institutions that give structure

[1] Cf. Paul VI, Encyclical Letter *Populorum Progressio* (26th March 1967), 22: *AAS* 59 (1967), 268; Second Vatican Ecumenical Council, Pastoral Constitution on the Church in the Modern World *Gaudium et Spes*, 69.

[2] *Address for the Day of Development* (23rd August 1968): *AAS* 60 (1968), 626-627.

[3] Cf. John Paul II, *Message for the 2002 World Day of Peace*: *AAS* 94 (2002), 132-140.

[4] Cf. Second Vatican Ecumenical Council, Pastoral Constitution on the Church in the Modern World *Gaudium et Spes*, 26.

to the life of society, juridically, civilly, politically and culturally, making it the *pólis*, or "city". The more we strive to secure a common good corresponding to the real needs of our neighbours, the more effectively we love them. Every Christian is called to practise this charity, in a manner corresponding to his vocation and according to the degree of influence he wields in the *pólis*. This is the institutional path - we might also call it the political path - of charity, no less excellent and effective than the kind of charity which encounters the neighbour directly, outside the institutional mediation of the *pólis*. When animated by charity, commitment to the common good has greater worth than a merely secular and political stand would have. Like all commitment to justice, it has a place within the testimony of divine charity that paves the way for eternity through temporal action. Man's earthly activity, when inspired and sustained by charity, contributes to the building of the universal *city of God*, which is the goal of the history of the human family. In an increasingly globalised society, the common good and the effort to obtain it cannot fail to assume the dimensions of the whole human family, that is to say, the community of peoples and nations,[5] in such a way as to shape the *earthly city* in unity and peace, rendering it to some degree an anticipation and a prefiguration of the undivided *city of God*.

8. In 1967, when he issued the Encyclical *Populorum Progressio*, my venerable predecessor Pope Paul VI illuminated the great theme of the development of peoples with the splendour of truth and the gentle light of Christ's charity. He taught that life in Christ is the first and principal factor of development[6] and he entrusted us with the task of travelling the path of development with all our heart and all our intelligence,[7] that is to say with the ardour of charity and the wisdom of truth. It is the primordial truth of God's love, grace bestowed upon us, that opens our lives to gift and makes it possible

---

[5] Cf. John XXIII, Encyclical Letter *Pacem in Terris* (11th April 1963): *AAS* 55 (1963), 268-270.

[6] Cf. no. 16: *loc. cit.*, 265.

[7] Cf. *ibid.*, 82: *loc. cit.*, 297.

to hope for a "development of the whole man and of all men,"[8] to hope for progress "from less human conditions to those which are more human",[9] obtained by overcoming the difficulties that are inevitably encountered along the way.

At a distance of over forty years from the Encyclical's publication, I intend to pay tribute and to honour the memory of the great Pope Paul VI, revisiting his teachings on *integral human development* and taking my place within the path that they marked out, so as to apply them to the present moment. This continual application to contemporary circumstances began with the Encyclical *Sollicitudo Rei Socialis*, with which the Servant of God Pope John Paul II chose to mark the twentieth anniversary of the publication of *Populorum Progressio*. Until that time, only *Rerum Novarum* had been commemorated in this way. Now that a further twenty years have passed, I express my conviction that *Populorum Progressio* deserves to be considered "the *Rerum Novarum* of the present age", shedding light upon humanity's journey towards unity.

9. Love in truth - *caritas in veritate* - is a great challenge for the Church in a world that is becoming progressively and pervasively globalised. The risk for our time is that the *de facto* interdependence of people and nations is not matched by ethical interaction of consciences and minds that would give rise to truly human development. Only in *charity, illumined by the light of reason and faith*, is it possible to pursue development goals that possess a more humane and humanising value. The sharing of goods and resources, from which authentic development proceeds, is not guaranteed by merely technical progress and relationships of utility, but by the potential of love that overcomes evil with good (cf. *Rm* 12:21), opening up the path towards reciprocity of consciences and liberties.

---

[8] *Ibid.*, 42: *loc. cit.*, 278.

[9] *Ibid.*, 20: *loc. cit.*, 267.

The Church does not have technical solutions to offer[10] and does not claim "to interfere in any way in the politics of States."[11] She does, however, have a mission of truth to accomplish, in every time and circumstance, for a society that is attuned to man, to his dignity, to his vocation. Without truth, it is easy to fall into an empiricist and sceptical view of life, incapable of rising to the level of praxis because of a lack of interest in grasping the values - sometimes even the meanings - with which to judge and direct it. Fidelity to man requires *fidelity to the truth*, which alone is the *guarantee of freedom* (cf. *Jn* 8:32) and of *the possibility of integral human development.* For this reason the Church searches for truth, proclaims it tirelessly and recognises it wherever it is manifested. This mission of truth is something that the Church can never renounce. Her social doctrine is a particular dimension of this proclamation: it is a service to the truth which sets us free. Open to the truth, from whichever branch of knowledge it comes, the Church's social doctrine receives it, assembles into a unity the fragments in which it is often found, and mediates it within the constantly changing life-patterns of the society of peoples and nations.[12]

---

[10] Cf. Second Vatican Ecumenical Council, Pastoral Constitution on the Church in the Modern World *Gaudium et Spes*, 36; Paul VI, Apostolic Letter *Octogesima Adveniens* (14th May 1971), 4: *AAS* 63 (1971), 403-404; John Paul II, Encyclical Letter *Centesimus Annus* (1st May 1991), 43: *AAS* 83 (1991), 847.

[11] Paul VI, Encyclical Letter *Populorum Progressio*, 13: *loc. cit.*, 263-264.

[12] Cf. Pontifical Council for Justice and Peace, *Compendium of the Social Doctrine of the Church*, 76.

CHAPTER ONE

THE MESSAGE OF *POPULORUM PROGRESSIO*

10. A fresh reading of *Populorum Progressio*, more than forty years after its publication, invites us to remain faithful to its message of charity and truth, viewed within the overall context of Paul VI's specific magisterium and, more generally, within the tradition of the Church's social doctrine. Moreover, an evaluation is needed of the different terms in which the problem of development is presented today, as compared with forty years ago. The correct viewpoint, then, is that of the *Tradition of the apostolic faith*,[13] a patrimony both ancient and new, outside of which *Populorum Progressio* would be a document without roots - and issues concerning development would be reduced to merely sociological data.

11. The publication of *Populorum Progressio* occurred immediately after the conclusion of the Second Vatican Ecumenical Council, and in its opening paragraphs it clearly indicates its close connection with the Council.[14] Twenty years later, in *Sollicitudo Rei Socialis,* John Paul II, in his turn, emphasised the earlier Encyclical's fruitful relationship with the Council, and especially with the Pastoral Constitution *Gaudium et Spes.*[15] I too wish to recall here the importance of the Second Vatican Council for Paul VI's Encyclical and for the whole of the subsequent social Magisterium of the Popes. The Council probed more deeply what had always belonged to the truth of the faith, namely that the Church, being at God's service, is at the service of the world in terms of love and truth. Paul VI set out from this vision in order to convey two important truths. The first is that *the whole Church, in all her being and acting - when she proclaims, when*

---

[13] Cf. Benedict XVI, *Address at the Inauguration of the Fifth General Conference of the Bishops of Latin America and the Caribbean* (Aparecida, 13th May 2007).

[14] Cf. nos. 3-5: *loc. cit.,* 258-260.

[15] Cf. John Paul II, Encyclical Letter *Sollicitudo Rei Socialis* (30th December 1987), 6-7: *AAS* 80 (1988), 517-519.

she celebrates, when she performs works of charity - is engaged in promoting integral human development. She has a public role over and above her charitable and educational activities: all the energy she brings to the advancement of humanity and of universal fraternity is manifested when she is able to operate in a climate of freedom. In not a few cases, that freedom is impeded by prohibitions and persecutions, or it is limited when the Church's public presence is reduced to her charitable activities alone. The second truth is that *authentic human development concerns the whole of the person in every single dimension.*[16] Without the perspective of eternal life, human progress in this world is denied breathing-space. Enclosed within history, it runs the risk of being reduced to the mere accumulation of wealth; humanity thus loses the courage to be at the service of higher goods, at the service of the great and disinterested initiatives called forth by universal charity. Man does not develop through his own powers, nor can development simply be handed to him. In the course of history, it was often maintained that the creation of institutions was sufficient to guarantee the fulfilment of humanity's right to development. Unfortunately, too much confidence was placed in those institutions, as if they were able to deliver the desired objective automatically. In reality, institutions by themselves are not enough, because integral human development is primarily a vocation, and therefore it involves a free assumption of responsibility in solidarity on the part of everyone. Moreover, such development requires a transcendent vision of the person, it needs God: without him, development is either denied, or entrusted exclusively to man, who falls into the trap of thinking he can bring about his own salvation, and ends up promoting a dehumanised form of development. Only through an encounter with God are we able to see in the other something more than just another creature,[17] to recognise the divine image in the other, thus truly coming to discover him or her and to mature in a love that "becomes concern and care for the other."[18]

---

[16] Cf. Paul VI, Encyclical Letter *Populorum Progressio*, 14: *loc. cit.*, 264.

[17] Cf. Benedict XVI, Encyclical Letter *Deus Caritas Est* (25th December 2005), 18: *AAS* 98 (2006), 232.

[18] *Ibid.*, 6: *loc cit.*, 222.

12. The link between *Populorum Progressio* and the Second Vatican Council does not mean that Paul VI's social magisterium marked a break with that of previous Popes, because the Council constitutes a deeper exploration of this magisterium within the continuity of the Church's life.[19] In this sense, clarity is not served by certain abstract subdivisions of the Church's social doctrine, which apply categories to Papal social teaching that are extraneous to it. It is not a case of two typologies of social doctrine, one pre-conciliar and one post-conciliar, differing from one another: on the contrary, there is *a single teaching, consistent and at the same time ever new*.[20] It is one thing to draw attention to the particular characteristics of one Encyclical or another, of the teaching of one Pope or another, but quite another to lose sight of the coherence of the overall doctrinal *corpus*.[21] Coherence does not mean a closed system: on the contrary, it means dynamic faithfulness to a light received. The Church's social doctrine illuminates with an unchanging light the new problems that are constantly emerging.[22] This safeguards the permanent and historical character of the doctrinal "patrimony"[23] which, with its specific characteristics, is part and parcel of the Church's ever-living Tradition.[24] Social doctrine is built on the foundation handed on by the Apostles to the Fathers of the Church, and then received and further explored by the great Christian doctors. This doctrine points definitively to the New Man, to the "last Adam [who] became a life-giving spirit" (1 *Co* 15:45), the principle of the charity that "never ends" (1 *Co* 13:8). It is attested by the saints and by those who gave their lives for Christ our Saviour in the field of justice and peace. It is an expression of the prophetic task of the Supreme Pontiffs to give apostolic guidance to the Church of Christ and to discern

[19] Cf. Benedict XVI, *Christmas Address to the Roman Curia*, 22nd December 2005.

[20] Cf. John Paul II, Encyclical Letter *Sollicitudo Rei Socialis*, 3: *loc. cit.*, 515.

[21] Cf. *ibid.*, 1: *loc. cit.*, 513-514.

[22] Cf. *ibid.*, 3: *loc. cit.*, 515.

[23] Cf. John Paul II, Encyclical Letter *Laborem Exercens* (14th September 1981), 3: *AAS* 73 (1981), 583-584.

[24] Cf. John Paul II, Encyclical Letter *Centesimus Annus*, 3: *loc. cit.*, 794-796.

the new demands of evangelisation. For these reasons, *Populorum Progressio*, situated within the great current of Tradition, can still speak to us today.

13. In addition to its important link with the entirety of the Church's social doctrine, *Populorum Progressio* is *closely connected to the overall magisterium of Paul VI*, especially his social magisterium. His was certainly a social teaching of great importance: he underlined the indispensable importance of the Gospel for building a society according to freedom and justice, in the ideal and historical perspective of a civilisation animated by love. Paul VI clearly understood that the social question had become worldwide[25] and he grasped the interconnection between the impetus towards the unification of humanity and the Christian ideal of a single family of peoples in solidarity and fraternity. *In the notion of development, understood in human and Christian terms, he identified the heart of the Christian social message*, and he proposed Christian charity as the principal force at the service of development. Motivated by the wish to make Christ's love fully visible to contemporary men and women, Paul VI addressed important ethical questions robustly, without yielding to the cultural weaknesses of his time.

14. In his Apostolic Letter *Octogesima Adveniens* of 1971, Paul VI reflected on the meaning of politics, and the *danger constituted by utopian and ideological visions* that place its ethical and human dimensions in jeopardy. These are matters closely connected with development. Unfortunately the negative ideologies continue to flourish. Paul VI had already warned against the technocratic ideology so prevalent today,[26] fully aware of the great danger of entrusting the entire process of development to technology alone, because in that way it would lack direction. Technology, viewed in itself, is ambivalent. If on the one hand, some today would be inclined to entrust the entire process of development to technology,

---

[25] Cf. Encyclical Letter *Populorum Progressio*, 3: *loc. cit.*, 258.

[26] Cf. *ibid.*, 34: *loc. cit.*, 274.

on the other hand we are witnessing an upsurge of ideologies that deny *in toto* the very value of development, viewing it as radically anti-human and merely a source of degradation. This leads to a rejection, not only of the distorted and unjust way in which progress is sometimes directed, but also of scientific discoveries themselves, which, if well used, could serve as an opportunity of growth for all. The idea of a world without development indicates a lack of trust in man and in God. It is therefore a serious mistake to undervalue human capacity to exercise control over the deviations of development or to overlook the fact that man is constitutionally oriented towards "being more". Idealising technical progress, or contemplating the utopia of a return to humanity's original natural state, are two contrasting ways of detaching progress from its moral evaluation and hence from our responsibility.

15. Two further documents by Paul VI without any direct link to social doctrine - the Encyclical *Humanae Vitae* (25th July 1968) and the Apostolic Exhortation *Evangelii Nuntiandi* (8th December 1975) - are highly important for delineating the *fully human meaning of the development that the Church proposes*. It is therefore helpful to consider these texts too in relation to *Populorum Progressio*.

The Encyclical *Humanae Vitae* emphasises both the unitive and the procreative meaning of sexuality, thereby locating at the foundation of society the married couple, man and woman, who accept one another mutually, in distinction and in complementarity: a couple, therefore, that is open to life.[27] This is not a question of purely individual morality: *Humanae Vitae* indicates the *strong links between life ethics and social ethics*, ushering in a new area of magisterial teaching that has gradually been articulated in a series of documents, most recently John Paul II's Encyclical *Evangelium Vitae*.[28] The Church forcefully maintains this link between life ethics and social ethics, fully aware that "a society lacks solid

---

[27] Cf. nos. 8-9: *AAS* 60 (1968), 485-487; Benedict XVI, *Address to the participants at the International Congress promoted by the Pontifical Lateran University on the fortieth anniversary of Paul VI's Encyclical "Humanae Vitae"*, 10th May 2008.

[28] Cf. Encyclical Letter *Evangelium Vitae* (25th March 1995), 93: *AAS* 87 (1995), 507-508.

foundations when, on the one hand, it asserts values such as the dignity of the person, justice and peace, but then, on the other hand, radically acts to the contrary by allowing or tolerating a variety of ways in which human life is devalued and violated, especially where it is weak or marginalised."[29]

The Apostolic Exhortation *Evangelii Nuntiandi*, for its part, is very closely linked with development, given that, in Paul VI's words, "evangelisation would not be complete if it did not take account of the unceasing interplay of the Gospel and of man's concrete life, both personal and social."[30] "Between evangelisation and human advancement - development and liberation - there are in fact profound links:"[31] on the basis of this insight, Paul VI clearly presented the relationship between the proclamation of Christ and the advancement of the individual in society. *Testimony to Christ's charity, through works of justice, peace and development, is part and parcel of evangelisation*, because Jesus Christ, who loves us, is concerned with the whole person. These important teachings form the basis for the missionary aspect[32] of the Church's social doctrine, which is an essential element of evangelisation.[33] The Church's social doctrine proclaims and bears witness to faith. It is an instrument and an indispensable setting for formation in faith.

16. In *Populorum Progressio*, Paul VI taught that progress, in its origin and essence, is first and foremost a *vocation*: "in the design of God, every man is called upon to develop and fulfil himself, for every life is a vocation."[34] This is what gives legitimacy to the Church's involvement in the whole question of development. If development were concerned with merely technical aspects of human life, and not with the meaning of man's pilgrimage through

[29] *Ibid.*, 101: *loc. cit.*, 516-518.

[30] No. 29: *AAS* 68 (1976), 25.

[31] *Ibid.*, 31: *loc. cit.*, 26.

[32] Cf. John Paul II, Encyclical Letter *Sollicitudo Rei Socialis*, 41: *loc. cit.*, 570-572.

[33] Cf. *ibid.*; Id., Encyclical Letter *Centesimus Annus*, 5, 54: *loc. cit.*, 799, 859-860.

[34] No. 15: *loc. cit.*, 265.

history in company with his fellow human beings, nor with identifying the goal of that journey, then the Church would not be entitled to speak on it. Paul VI, like Leo XIII before him in *Rerum Novarum*,[35] knew that he was carrying out a duty proper to his office by shedding the light of the Gospel on the social questions of his time.[36]

To regard *development as a vocation* is to recognise, on the one hand, that it derives from a transcendent call, and on the other hand that it is incapable, on its own, of supplying its ultimate meaning. Not without reason the word "vocation" is also found in another passage of the Encyclical, where we read: "There is no true humanism but that which is open to the Absolute, and is conscious of a vocation which gives human life its true meaning."[37] This vision of development is at the heart of *Populorum Progressio*, and it lies behind all Paul VI's reflections on freedom, on truth and on charity in development. It is also the principal reason why that Encyclical is still timely in our day.

17. A vocation is a call that requires a free and responsible answer. *Integral human development presupposes the responsible freedom of the individual and of peoples*: no structure can guarantee this development over and above human responsibility. The "types of messianism which give promises but create illusions"[38] always build their case on a denial of the transcendent dimension of development, in the conviction that it lies entirely at their disposal. This false security becomes a weakness, because it involves reducing man to subservience, to a mere means for development, while the humility of those who accept a vocation is transformed into true autonomy, because it sets them free. Paul VI was in no doubt that obstacles and

---

[35] Cf. *ibid.*, 2: *loc. cit.*, 258; Leo XIII, Encyclical Letter *Rerum Novarum* (15th May 1891): *Leonis XIII P.M. Acta*, XI, Romae 1892, 97-144; John Paul II, Encyclical Letter *Sollicitudo Rei Socialis*, 8: *loc. cit.*, 519-520; Id., Encyclical Letter *Centesimus Annus*, 5: *loc. cit.*, 799.

[36] Cf. Encyclical Letter *Populorum Progressio*, 2, 13: *loc. cit.*, 258, 263-264.

[37] *Ibid.*, 42: *loc. cit.*, 278.

[38] *Ibid.*, 11: *loc. cit.*, 262; cf. John Paul II, Encyclical Letter *Centesimus Annus*, 25: *loc. cit.*, 822-824.

forms of conditioning hold up development, but he was also certain that "each one remains, whatever be these influences affecting him, the principal agent of his own success or failure."[39] This freedom concerns the type of development we are considering, but it also affects situations of underdevelopment which are not due to chance or historical necessity, but are attributable to human responsibility. This is why "the peoples in hunger are making a dramatic appeal to the peoples blessed with abundance."[40] This too is a vocation, a call addressed by free subjects to other free subjects in favour of an assumption of shared responsibility. Paul VI had a keen sense of the importance of economic structures and institutions, but he had an equally clear sense of their nature as instruments of human freedom. Only when it is free can development be integrally human; only in a climate of responsible freedom can it grow in a satisfactory manner.

18. Besides requiring freedom, *integral human development as a vocation also demands respect for its truth.* The vocation to progress drives us to "do more, know more and have more in order to be more."[41] But herein lies the problem: what does it mean "to be more"? Paul VI answers the question by indicating the essential quality of "authentic" development: it must be "integral, that is, it has to promote the good of every man and of the whole man."[42] Amid the various competing anthropological visions put forward in today's society, even more so than in Paul VI's time, the Christian vision has the particular characteristic of asserting and justifying the unconditional value of the human person and the meaning of his growth. The Christian vocation to development helps to promote the advancement of all men and of the whole man. As Paul VI wrote: "What we hold important is man, each man and each group of men, and we even include the whole of

[39] Encyclical Letter *Populorum Progressio*, 15: *loc. cit.*, 265.
[40] *Ibid.*, 3: *loc. cit.*, 258.
[41] *Ibid.*, 6: *loc. cit.*, 260.
[42] *Ibid.*, 14: *loc. cit.*, 264.

humanity."[43] In promoting development, the Christian faith does not rely on privilege or positions of power, nor even on the merits of Christians (even though these existed and continue to exist alongside their natural limitations),[44] but only on Christ, to whom every authentic vocation to integral human development must be directed. *The Gospel is fundamental for development*, because in the Gospel, Christ, "in the very revelation of the mystery of the Father and of his love, fully reveals humanity to itself."[45] Taught by her Lord, the Church examines the signs of the times and interprets them, offering the world "what she possesses as her characteristic attribute: a global vision of man and of the human race".[46] Precisely because God gives a resounding "yes" to man,[47] man cannot fail to open himself to the divine vocation to pursue his own development. The truth of development consists in its completeness: if it does not involve the whole man and every man, it is not true development. This is the central message of *Populorum Progressio*, valid for today and for all time. Integral human development on the natural plane, as a response to a vocation from God the Creator,[48] demands self-fulfilment in a "transcendent humanism which gives [to man] his greatest possible perfection: this is the highest goal of personal development."[49] The Christian vocation to this development therefore applies to both the natural plane and the supernatural plane; which is why, "when God is eclipsed, our ability to recognise the natural order, purpose and the 'good' begins to wane."[50]

---

[43] *Ibid.*; cf. John Paul II, Encyclical Letter *Centesimus Annus*, 53-62: *loc. cit.*, 859-867; Id., Encyclical Letter *Redemptor Hominis* (4th March 1979), 13-14: *AAS* 71 (1979), 282-286.

[44] Cf. Paul VI, Encyclical Letter *Populorum Progressio*, 12: *loc. cit.*, 262-263.

[45] Second Vatican Ecumenical Council, Pastoral Constitution on the Church in the Modern World *Gaudium et Spes*, 22.

[46] Paul VI, Encyclical Letter *Populorum Progressio*, 13: *loc. cit.*, 263-264.

[47] Cf. Benedict XVI, *Address to the Participants in the Fourth National Congress of the Church in Italy,* Verona, 19th October 2006.

[48] Cf. Paul VI, Encyclical Letter *Populorum Progressio*, 16: *loc. cit.*, 265.

[49] *Ibid.*

[50] Benedict XVI, *Address to young people at Barangaroo*, Sydney, 17th July 2008.

19. Finally, the vision of development as a vocation brings with it the *central place of charity within that development*. Paul VI, in his Encyclical Letter *Populorum Progressio*, pointed out that the causes of underdevelopment are not primarily of the material order. He invited us to search for them in other dimensions of the human person: first of all, in the will, which often neglects the duties of solidarity; secondly in thinking, which does not always give proper direction to the will. Hence, in the pursuit of development, there is a need for "the deep thought and reflection of wise men in search of a new humanism which will enable modern man to find himself anew."[51] But that is not all. Underdevelopment has an even more important cause than lack of deep thought: it is "the lack of brotherhood among individuals and peoples."[52] Will it ever be possible to obtain this brotherhood by human effort alone? As society becomes ever more globalised, it makes us neighbours but does not make us brothers. Reason, by itself, is capable of grasping the equality between men and of giving stability to their civic coexistence, but it cannot establish fraternity. This originates in a transcendent vocation from God the Father, who loved us first, teaching us through the Son what fraternal charity is. Paul VI, presenting the various levels in the process of human development, placed at the summit, after mentioning faith, "unity in the charity of Christ who calls us all to share as sons in the life of the living God, the Father of all."[53]

20. These perspectives, which *Populorum Progressio* opens up, remain fundamental for giving breathing-space and direction to our commitment for the development of peoples. Moreover, *Populorum Progressio* repeatedly underlines the *urgent need for reform*,[54] and in the face of great problems of injustice in the development of peoples, it calls for courageous action to be taken without delay.

---

[51] Paul VI, Encyclical Letter *Populorum Progressio*, 20: *loc. cit.*, 267.

[52] *Ibid.*, 66: *loc. cit.*, 289-290.

[53] *Ibid.*, 21: *loc. cit.*, 267-268.

[54] Cf. nos. 3, 29, 32: *loc. cit.*, 258, 272, 273.

This *urgency is also a consequence of charity in truth.* It is Christ's charity that drives us on: *"caritas Christi urget nos"* (2 *Co* 5:14). The urgency is inscribed not only in things, it is not derived solely from the rapid succession of events and problems, but also from the very matter that is at stake: the establishment of authentic fraternity. The importance of this goal is such as to demand our openness to understand it in depth and to mobilise ourselves at the level of the "heart", so as to ensure that current economic and social processes evolve towards fully human outcomes.

CHAPTER TWO

HUMAN DEVELOPMENT IN OUR TIME

21. Paul VI had an *articulated vision of development*. He understood the term to indicate the goal of rescuing peoples, first and foremost, from hunger, deprivation, endemic diseases and illiteracy. From the economic point of view, this meant their active participation, on equal terms, in the international economic process; from the social point of view, it meant their evolution into educated societies marked by solidarity; from the political point of view, it meant the consolidation of democratic regimes capable of ensuring freedom and peace. After so many years, as we observe with concern the developments and perspectives of the succession of crises that afflict the world today, *we ask to what extent Paul VI's expectations have been fulfilled* by the model of development adopted in recent decades. We recognise, therefore, that the Church had good reason to be concerned about the capacity of a purely technological society to set realistic goals and to make good use of the instruments at its disposal. Profit is useful if it serves as a means towards an end that provides a sense both of how to produce it and how to make good use of it. Once profit becomes the exclusive goal, if it is produced by improper means and without the common good as its ultimate end, it risks destroying wealth and creating poverty. The economic development that Paul VI hoped to see was meant to produce real growth, of benefit to everyone and genuinely sustainable. It is true that growth has taken place, and it continues to be a positive factor that has lifted billions of people out of misery - recently it has given many countries the possibility of becoming effective players in international politics. Yet it must be acknowledged that this same economic growth has been and continues to be weighed down by *malfunctions and dramatic problems*, highlighted even further by the current crisis. This presents us with choices that cannot be postponed concerning nothing less than the destiny of man, who, moreover, cannot prescind from his nature. The technical forces

in play, the global interrelations, the damaging effects on the real economy of badly managed and largely speculative financial dealing, large-scale migration of peoples, often provoked by some particular circumstance and then given insufficient attention, the unregulated exploitation of the earth's resources: all this leads us today to reflect on the measures that would be necessary to provide a solution to problems that are not only new in comparison to those addressed by Pope Paul VI, but also, and above all, of decisive impact upon the present and future good of humanity. The different aspects of the crisis, its solutions, and any new development that the future may bring, are increasingly interconnected, they imply one another, they require new efforts of holistic understanding and a *new humanistic synthesis*. The complexity and gravity of the present economic situation rightly cause us concern, but we must adopt a realistic attitude as we take up with confidence and hope the new responsibilities to which we are called by the prospect of a world in need of profound cultural renewal, a world that needs to rediscover fundamental values on which to build a better future. The current crisis obliges us to re-plan our journey, to set ourselves new rules and to discover new forms of commitment, to build on positive experiences and to reject negative ones. The crisis thus becomes *an opportunity for discernment, in which to shape a new vision for the future*. In this spirit, with confidence rather than resignation, it is appropriate to address the difficulties of the present time.

22. Today the picture of development has *many overlapping layers*. The actors and the causes in both underdevelopment and development are manifold, the faults and the merits are differentiated. This fact should prompt us to liberate ourselves from ideologies, which often oversimplify reality in artificial ways, and it should lead us to examine objectively the full human dimension of the problems. As John Paul II has already observed, the demarcation line between

rich and poor countries is no longer as clear as it was at the time of *Populorum Progressio*.[55] *The world's wealth is growing in absolute terms, but inequalities are on the increase*. In rich countries, new sectors of society are succumbing to poverty and new forms of poverty are emerging. In poorer areas some groups enjoy a sort of "superdevelopment" of a wasteful and consumerist kind which forms an unacceptable contrast with the ongoing situations of dehumanising deprivation. "The scandal of glaring inequalities"[56] continues. Corruption and illegality are unfortunately evident in the conduct of the economic and political class in rich countries, both old and new, as well as in poor ones. Among those who sometimes fail to respect the human rights of workers are large multinational companies as well as local producers. International aid has often been diverted from its proper ends, through irresponsible actions both within the chain of donors and within that of the beneficiaries. Similarly, in the context of immaterial or cultural causes of development and underdevelopment, we find these same patterns of responsibility reproduced. On the part of rich countries there is excessive zeal for protecting knowledge through an unduly rigid assertion of the right to intellectual property, especially in the field of health care. At the same time, in some poor countries, cultural models and social norms of behaviour persist which hinder the process of development.

23. Many areas of the globe today have evolved considerably, albeit in problematical and disparate ways, thereby taking their place among the great powers destined to play important roles in the future. Yet it should be stressed that *progress of a merely economic and technological kind is insufficient*. Development needs above all to be true and integral. The mere fact of emerging from economic backwardness, though positive in itself, does not resolve the complex issues of human advancement, neither for the countries that are spearheading such progress, nor for those that are

---

[55] Cf. Encyclical Letter, *Sollicitudo Rei Socialis*, 28: *loc. cit.*, 548-550.

[56] Paul VI, Encyclical Letter *Populorum Progressio*, 9: *loc. cit.*, 261-262.

already economically developed, nor even for those that are still poor, which can suffer not just through old forms of exploitation, but also from the negative consequences of a growth that is marked by irregularities and imbalances.

After the collapse of the economic and political systems of the Communist countries of Eastern Europe and the end of the so-called *opposing blocs*, a complete re-examination of development was needed. Pope John Paul II called for it, when in 1987 he pointed to the existence of these blocs as one of the principal causes of underdevelopment,[57] inasmuch as politics withdrew resources from the economy and from the culture, and ideology inhibited freedom. Moreover, in 1991, after the events of 1989, he asked that, in view of the ending of the blocs, there should be a comprehensive new plan for development, not only in those countries, but also in the West and in those parts of the world that were in the process of evolving.[58] This has been achieved only in part, and it is still a real duty that needs to be discharged, perhaps by means of the choices that are necessary to overcome current economic problems.

24. The world that Paul VI had before him - even though society had already evolved to such an extent that he could speak of social issues in global terms - was still far less integrated than today's world. Economic activity and the political process were both largely conducted within the same geographical area, and could therefore feed off one another. Production took place predominantly within national boundaries, and financial investments had somewhat limited circulation outside the country, so that the politics of many States could still determine the priorities of the economy and to some degree govern its performance using the instruments at their disposal. Hence *Populorum Progressio* assigned a central, albeit not exclusive, role to "public authorities".[59]

---

[57] Cf. Encyclical Letter *Sollicitudo Rei Socialis*, 20: *loc. cit.*, 536-537.

[58] Cf. John Paul II, Encyclical Letter *Centesimus Annus*, 22-29: *loc. cit.*, 819-830.

[59] Cf. nos. 23, 33: *loc. cit.*, 268-269, 273-274.

In our own day, the State finds itself having to address the limitations to its sovereignty imposed by the new context of international trade and finance, which is characterised by increasing mobility both of financial capital and means of production, material and immaterial. This new context has altered the political power of States.

Today, as we take to heart the lessons of the current economic crisis, which sees the State's *public authorities* directly involved in correcting errors and malfunctions, it seems more realistic to *re-evaluate their role* and their powers, which need to be prudently reviewed and remodelled so as to enable them, perhaps through new forms of engagement, to address the challenges of today's world. Once the role of public authorities has been more clearly defined, one could foresee an increase in the new forms of political participation, nationally and internationally, that have come about through the activity of organisations operating in civil society; in this way it is to be hoped that the citizens' interest and participation in the *res publica* will become more deeply rooted.

25. From the social point of view, systems of protection and welfare, already present in many countries in Paul VI's day, are finding it hard and could find it even harder in the future to pursue their goals of true social justice in today's profoundly changed environment. The global market has stimulated first and foremost, on the part of rich countries, a search for areas in which to outsource production at low cost with a view to reducing the prices of many goods, increasing purchasing power and thus accelerating the rate of development in terms of greater availability of consumer goods for the domestic market. Consequently, the market has prompted new forms of competition between States as they seek to attract foreign businesses to set up production centres, by means of a variety of instruments, including favourable fiscal regimes and deregulation of the labour market. These processes have led to a *downsizing of social security systems* as the price to be paid for seeking greater competitive advantage in the global market, with consequent grave danger for the rights of workers, for fundamental human rights and for the solidarity associated with the traditional forms of the social

State. Systems of social security can lose the capacity to carry out their task, both in emerging countries and in those that were among the earliest to develop, as well as in poor countries. Here budgetary policies, with cuts in social spending often made under pressure from international financial institutions, can leave citizens powerless in the face of old and new risks; such powerlessness is increased by the lack of effective protection on the part of workers' associations. Through the combination of social and economic change, *trade union organisations* experience greater difficulty in carrying out their task of representing the interests of workers, partly because Governments, for reasons of economic utility, often limit the freedom or the negotiating capacity of labour unions. Hence traditional networks of solidarity have more and more obstacles to overcome. The repeated calls issued within the Church's social doctrine, beginning with *Rerum Novarum*,[60] for the promotion of workers' associations that can defend their rights must therefore be honoured today even more than in the past, as a prompt and far-sighted response to the urgent need for new forms of cooperation at the international level, as well as the local level.

The *mobility of labour*, associated with a climate of deregulation, is an important phenomenon with certain positive aspects, because it can stimulate wealth production and cultural exchange. Nevertheless, uncertainty over working conditions caused by mobility and deregulation, when it becomes endemic, tends to create new forms of psychological instability, giving rise to difficulty in forging coherent life-plans, including that of marriage. This leads to situations of human decline, to say nothing of the waste of social resources. In comparison with the casualties of industrial society in the past, unemployment today provokes new forms of economic marginalisation, and the current crisis can only make this situation worse. Being out of work or dependent on public or private assistance for a prolonged period undermines the freedom and creativity of the person and his family and social relationships, causing great psychological and spiritual suffering. I would like to remind everyone, especially governments

[60] Cf. *loc. cit.*, 135.

engaged in boosting the world's economic and social assets, that the *primary capital to be safeguarded and valued is man, the human person in his or her integrity*: "Man is the source, the focus and the aim of all economic and social life."[61]

26. On the cultural plane, compared with Paul VI's day, the difference is even more marked. At that time cultures were relatively well defined and had greater opportunity to defend themselves against attempts to merge them into one. Today the possibilities of *interaction between cultures* have increased significantly, giving rise to new openings for intercultural dialogue: a dialogue that, if it is to be effective, has to set out from a deep-seated knowledge of the specific identity of the various dialogue partners. Let it not be forgotten that the increased commercialisation of cultural exchange today leads to a twofold danger. First, one may observe a *cultural eclecticism* that is often assumed uncritically: cultures are simply placed alongside one another and viewed as substantially equivalent and interchangeable. This easily yields to a relativism that does not serve true intercultural dialogue; on the social plane, cultural relativism has the effect that cultural groups coexist side by side, but remain separate, with no authentic dialogue and therefore with no true integration. Secondly, the opposite danger exists, that of *cultural levelling* and indiscriminate acceptance of types of conduct and life-styles. In this way one loses sight of the profound significance of the culture of different nations, of the traditions of the various peoples, by which the individual defines himself in relation to life's fundamental questions.[62] What eclecticism and cultural levelling have in common is the separation of culture from human nature. Thus, cultures can no longer define themselves within a nature that transcends them,[63] and man ends up being

---

[61] Second Vatican Ecumenical Council, Pastoral Constitution on the Church in the Modern World *Gaudium et Spes*, 63.

[62] Cf. John Paul II, Encyclical Letter *Centesimus Annus*, 24: *loc. cit.*, 821-822.

[63] Cf. John Paul II, Encyclical Letter *Veritatis Splendor* (6th August 1993), 33, 46, 51: *AAS* 85 (1993), 1160, 1169-1171, 1174-1175; Id., *Address to the Assembly of the United Nations*, 5th October 1995, 3.

reduced to a mere cultural statistic. When this happens, humanity runs new risks of enslavement and manipulation.

27. Life in many poor countries is still extremely insecure as a consequence of food shortages, and the situation could become worse: *hunger* still reaps enormous numbers of victims among those who, like Lazarus, are not permitted to take their place at the rich man's table, contrary to the hopes expressed by Paul VI.[64] *Feed the hungry* (cf. *Mt* 25:35,37,42) is an ethical imperative for the universal Church, as she responds to the teachings of her Founder, the Lord Jesus, concerning solidarity and the sharing of goods. Moreover, the elimination of world hunger has also, in the global era, become a requirement for safeguarding the peace and stability of the planet. Hunger is not so much dependent on lack of material things as on shortage of social resources, the most important of which are institutional. What is missing, in other words, is a network of economic institutions capable of guaranteeing regular access to sufficient food and water for nutritional needs, and also capable of addressing the primary needs and necessities ensuing from genuine food crises, whether due to natural causes or political irresponsibility, nationally and internationally. The problem of food insecurity needs to be addressed within a long-term perspective, eliminating the structural causes that give rise to it and promoting the agricultural development of poorer countries. This can be done by investing in rural infrastructures, irrigation systems, transport, organisation of markets, and in the development and dissemination of agricultural technology that can make the best use of the human, natural and socio-economic resources that are more readily available at the local level, while guaranteeing their sustainability over the long term as well. All this needs to be accomplished with the involvement of local communities in choices and decisions that affect the use of agricultural land. In this perspective, it could be useful to consider the new possibilities

---

[64] Cf. Encyclical Letter *Populorum Progressio*, 47: *loc. cit.*, 280-281; John Paul II, Encyclical Letter *Sollicitudo Rei Socialis*, 42: *loc. cit.*, 572-574.

that are opening up through proper use of traditional as well as innovative farming techniques, always assuming that these have been judged, after sufficient testing, to be appropriate, respectful of the environment and attentive to the needs of the most deprived peoples. At the same time, the question of equitable agrarian reform in developing countries should not be ignored. The right to food, like the right to water, has an important place within the pursuit of other rights, beginning with the fundamental right to life. It is therefore necessary to cultivate a public conscience that considers *food and access to water as universal rights of all human beings, without distinction or discrimination*.[65] It is important, moreover, to emphasise that solidarity with poor countries in the process of development can point towards a solution of the current global crisis, as politicians and directors of international institutions have begun to sense in recent times. Through support for economically poor countries by means of financial plans inspired by solidarity - so that these countries can take steps to satisfy their own citizens' demand for consumer goods and for development - not only can true economic growth be generated, but a contribution can be made towards sustaining the productive capacities of rich countries that risk being compromised by the crisis.

28. One of the most striking aspects of development in the present day is the important question of *respect for life*, which cannot in any way be detached from questions concerning the development of peoples. It is an aspect which has acquired increasing prominence in recent times, obliging us to broaden our concept of poverty[66] and underdevelopment to include questions connected with the acceptance of life, especially in cases where it is impeded in a variety of ways.

Not only does the situation of poverty still provoke high rates of infant mortality in many regions, but some parts of the world

---

[65] Cf. Benedict XVI, *Message for the 2007 World Food Day: AAS* 99 (2007), 933-935.

[66] Cf. John Paul II, Encyclical Letter *Evangelium Vitae*, 18, 59, 63-64: *loc. cit.*, 419-421, 467-468, 472-475.

still experience practices of demographic control, on the part of governments that often promote contraception and even go so far as to impose abortion. In economically developed countries, legislation contrary to life is very widespread, and it has already shaped moral attitudes and praxis, contributing to the spread of an anti-birth mentality; frequent attempts are made to export this mentality to other States as if it were a form of cultural progress.

Some non-governmental Organisations work actively to spread abortion, at times promoting the practice of sterilisation in poor countries, in some cases not even informing the women concerned. Moreover, there is reason to suspect that development aid is sometimes linked to specific health-care policies which *de facto* involve the imposition of strong birth control measures. Further grounds for concern are laws permitting euthanasia as well as pressure from lobby groups, nationally and internationally, in favour of its juridical recognition.

Openness to life is at the centre of true development. When a society moves towards the denial or suppression of life, it ends up no longer finding the necessary motivation and energy to strive for man's true good. If personal and social sensitivity towards the acceptance of a new life is lost, then other forms of acceptance that are valuable for society also wither away.[67] The acceptance of life strengthens moral fibre and makes people capable of mutual help. By cultivating openness to life, wealthy peoples can better understand the needs of poor ones, they can avoid employing huge economic and intellectual resources to satisfy the selfish desires of their own citizens, and instead, they can promote virtuous action within the perspective of production that is morally sound and marked by solidarity, respecting the fundamental right to life of every people and every individual.

29. There is another aspect of modern life that is very closely connected to development: the denial of the *right to religious freedom*. I am not referring simply to the struggles and conflicts

---

[67] Cf. Benedict XVI, *Message for the 2007 World Day of Peace*, 5.

that continue to be fought in the world for religious motives, even if at times the religious motive is merely a cover for other reasons, such as the desire for domination and wealth. Today, in fact, people frequently kill in the holy name of God, as both my predecessor John Paul II and I myself have often publicly acknowledged and lamented.[68] Violence puts the brakes on authentic development and impedes the evolution of peoples towards greater socio-economic and spiritual well-being. This applies especially to terrorism motivated by fundamentalism,[69] which generates grief, destruction and death, obstructs dialogue between nations and diverts extensive resources from their peaceful and civil uses.

Yet it should be added that, as well as religious fanaticism that in some contexts impedes the exercise of the right to religious freedom, so too the deliberate promotion of religious indifference or practical atheism on the part of many countries obstructs the requirements for the development of peoples, depriving them of spiritual and human resources. God is *the guarantor of man's true development*, inasmuch as, having created him in his image, he also establishes the transcendent dignity of men and women and feeds their innate yearning to "be more". Man is not a lost atom in a random universe:[70] he is God's creature, whom God chose to endow with an immortal soul and whom he has always loved. If man were merely the fruit of either chance or necessity, or if he had to lower his aspirations to the limited horizon of the world in which he lives, if all reality were merely history and culture, and man did not possess a nature destined to transcend itself in a supernatural life, then one could speak of growth, or evolution, but not development. When the State promotes, teaches, or actually imposes forms of practical atheism, it deprives its citizens of the moral and spiritual strength

---

[68] Cf. John Paul II, *Message for the 2002 World Day of Peace*, 4-7, 12-15: *AAS* 94 (2002), 134-136, 138-140; Id., *Message for the 2004 World Day of Peace*, 8: *AAS* 96 (2004), 119; Id., *Message for the 2005 World Day of Peace*, 4: *AAS* 97 (2005), 177-178; Benedict XVI, *Message for the 2006 World Day of Peace*, 9-10: *AAS* 98 (2006), 60-61; Id., *Message for the 2007 World Day of Peace*, 5, 14: *loc. cit.*, 778, 782-783.

[69] Cf. John Paul II, *Message for the 2002 World Day of Peace*, 6: *loc. cit.*, 135; Benedict XVI, *Message for the 2006 World Day of Peace*, 9-10: *loc. cit.*, 60-61.

[70] Cf. Benedict XVI, *Homily at Mass*, Islinger Feld, Regensburg, 12th September 2006.

that is indispensable for attaining integral human development and it impedes them from moving forward with renewed dynamism as they strive to offer a more generous human response to divine love.[71] In the context of cultural, commercial or political relations, it also sometimes happens that economically developed or emerging countries export this reductive vision of the person and his destiny to poor countries. This is the damage that "superdevelopment"[72] causes to authentic development when it is accompanied by "moral underdevelopment".[73]

30. In this context, the theme of integral human development takes on an even broader range of meanings: the correlation between its multiple elements requires a commitment to *foster the interaction of the different levels of human knowledge* in order to promote the authentic development of peoples. Often it is thought that development, or the socio-economic measures that go with it, merely require to be implemented through joint action. This joint action, however, needs to be given direction, because "all social action involves a doctrine."[74] In view of the complexity of the issues, it is obvious that the various disciplines have to work together through an orderly interdisciplinary exchange. Charity does not exclude knowledge, but rather requires, promotes, and animates it from within. Knowledge is never purely the work of the intellect. It can certainly be reduced to calculation and experiment, but if it aspires to be wisdom capable of directing man in the light of his first beginnings and his final ends, it must be "seasoned" with the "salt" of charity. Deeds without knowledge are blind, and knowledge without love is sterile. Indeed, "the individual who is animated by true charity labours skilfully to discover the causes of misery, to find the means to combat it, to overcome it resolutely."[75] Faced with the phenomena that lie before us, charity in truth requires

---

[71] Cf. Benedict XVI, Encyclical Letter *Deus Caritas Est*, 1: *loc. cit.*, 217-218.

[72] John Paul II, Encyclical Letter *Sollicitudo Rei Socialis*, 28: *loc. cit.*, 548-550.

[73] Paul VI, Encyclical Letter *Populorum Progressio*, 19: *loc. cit.*, 266-267.

[74] *Ibid.*, 39: *loc. cit.*, 276-277.

[75] *Ibid.*, 75: *loc. cit.*, 293-294.

first of all that we know and understand, acknowledging and respecting the specific competence of every level of knowledge. Charity is not an added extra, like an appendix to work already concluded in each of the various disciplines: it engages them in dialogue from the very beginning. The demands of love do not contradict those of reason. Human knowledge is insufficient and the conclusions of science cannot indicate by themselves the path towards integral human development. There is always a need to push further ahead: this is what is required by charity in truth.[76] Going beyond, however, never means prescinding from the conclusions of reason, nor contradicting its results. Intelligence and love are not in separate compartments: *love is rich in intelligence and intelligence is full of love*.

31. This means that moral evaluation and scientific research must go hand in hand, and that charity must animate them in a harmonious interdisciplinary whole, marked by unity and distinction. The Church's social doctrine, which has "*an important interdisciplinary dimension*",[77] can exercise, in this perspective, a function of extraordinary effectiveness. It allows faith, theology, metaphysics and science to come together in a collaborative effort in the service of humanity. It is here above all that the Church's social doctrine displays its dimension of wisdom. Paul VI had seen clearly that among the causes of underdevelopment there is a lack of wisdom and reflection, a lack of thinking capable of formulating a guiding synthesis,[78] for which "a clear vision of all economic, social, cultural and spiritual aspects"[79] is required. The excessive segmentation of knowledge,[80] the rejection of metaphysics by the human sciences,[81] the difficulties encountered by dialogue between

---

[76] Cf. Benedict XVI, Encyclical Letter *Deus Caritas Est*, 28: *loc. cit.*, 238-240.

[77] John Paul II, Encyclical Letter *Centesimus Annus*, 59: *loc. cit.*, 864.

[78] Cf. Encyclical Letter *Populorum Progressio*, 40, 85: *loc. cit.*, 277, 298-299.

[79] *Ibid.*, 13: *loc. cit.*, 263-264.

[80] Cf. John Paul II, Encyclical Letter *Fides et Ratio* (14th September 1998), 85: *AAS* 91 (1999), 72-73.

[81] Cf. *ibid.*, 83: *loc. cit.*, 70-71.

science and theology are damaging not only to the development of knowledge, but also to the development of peoples, because these things make it harder to see the integral good of man in its various dimensions. The "broadening [of] our concept of reason and its application"[82] is indispensable if we are to succeed in adequately weighing all the elements involved in the question of development and in the solution of socio-economic problems.

32. The significant new elements in the picture of the development of peoples today in many cases demand *new solutions*. These need to be found together, respecting the laws proper to each element and in the light of an integral vision of man, reflecting the different aspects of the human person, contemplated through a lens purified by charity. Remarkable convergences and possible solutions will then come to light, without any fundamental component of human life being obscured.

The dignity of the individual and the demands of justice require, particularly today, that economic choices do not cause disparities in wealth to increase in an excessive and morally unacceptable manner,[83] and that we continue to *prioritise the goal of access to steady employment* for everyone. All things considered, this is also required by "economic logic". Through the systemic increase of social inequality, both within a single country and between the populations of different countries (i.e. the massive increase in relative poverty), not only does social cohesion suffer, thereby placing democracy at risk, but so too does the economy, through the progressive erosion of "social capital": the network of relationships of trust, dependability, and respect for rules, all of which are indispensable for any form of civil coexistence.

Economic science tells us that structural insecurity generates anti-productive attitudes wasteful of human resources, inasmuch as workers tend to adapt passively to automatic mechanisms, rather than to release creativity. On this point too, there is a convergence

[82] Benedict XVI, *Address at the University of Regensburg*, 12th September 2006.
[83] Cf. Paul VI, Encyclical Letter *Populorum Progressio*, 33: *loc. cit.*, 273-274.

between economic science and moral evaluation. *Human costs always include economic costs*, and economic dysfunctions always involve human costs.

It should be remembered that the reduction of cultures to the technological dimension, even if it favours short-term profits, in the long term impedes reciprocal enrichment and the dynamics of cooperation. It is important to distinguish between short- and long-term economic or sociological considerations. Lowering the level of protection accorded to the rights of workers, or abandoning mechanisms of wealth redistribution in order to increase the country's international competitiveness, hinder the achievement of lasting development. Moreover, the human consequences of current tendencies towards a short-term economy - sometimes very short-term - need to be carefully evaluated. This requires *further and deeper reflection on the meaning of the economy and its goals,*[84] as well as a profound and far-sighted revision of the current model of development, so as to correct its dysfunctions and deviations. This is demanded, in any case, by the earth's state of ecological health; above all it is required by the cultural and moral crisis of man, the symptoms of which have been evident for some time all over the world.

33. More than forty years after *Populorum Progressio*, its basic theme, namely progress, *remains an open question*, made all the more acute and urgent by the current economic and financial crisis. If some areas of the globe, with a history of poverty, have experienced remarkable changes in terms of their economic growth and their share in world production, other zones are still living in a situation of deprivation comparable to that which existed at the time of Paul VI, and in some cases one can even speak of a deterioration. It is significant that some of the causes of this situation were identified in *Populorum Progressio*, such as the high tariffs imposed by economically developed countries, which still make it difficult for the products of poor countries to gain a foothold in the markets of rich countries. Other causes, however, mentioned only in passing

---

[84] Cf. John Paul II, *Message for the 2000 World Day of Peace*, 15: *AAS* 92 (2000), 366.

in the Encyclical, have since emerged with greater clarity. A case in point would be the evaluation of the process of decolonisation, then at its height. Paul VI hoped to see the journey towards autonomy unfold freely and in peace. More than forty years later, we must acknowledge how difficult this journey has been, both because of new forms of colonialism and continued dependence on old and new foreign powers, and because of grave irresponsibility within the very countries that have achieved independence.

The principal new feature has been the *explosion of worldwide interdependence*, commonly known as globalisation. Paul VI had partially foreseen it, but the ferocious pace at which it has evolved could not have been anticipated. Originating within economically developed countries, this process by its nature has spread to include all economies. It has been the principal driving force behind the emergence from underdevelopment of whole regions, and in itself it represents a great opportunity. Nevertheless, without the guidance of charity in truth, this global force could cause unprecedented damage and create new divisions within the human family. Hence charity and truth confront us with an altogether new and creative challenge, one that is certainly vast and complex. It is about *broadening the scope of reason and making it capable of knowing and directing these powerful new forces*, animating them within the perspective of that "civilization of love" whose seed God has planted in every people, in every culture.

CHAPTER THREE

FRATERNITY, ECONOMIC DEVELOPMENT
AND CIVIL SOCIETY

34. *Charity in truth* places man before the astonishing experience of
gift. Gratuitousness is present in our lives in many different forms,
which often go unrecognised because of a purely consumerist
and utilitarian view of life. The human being is made for gift,
which expresses and makes present his transcendent dimension.
Sometimes modern man is wrongly convinced that he is the sole
author of himself, his life and society. This is a presumption that
follows from being selfishly closed in upon himself, and it is a
consequence - to express it in faith terms - of *original sin*. The
Church's wisdom has always pointed to the presence of original sin
in social conditions and in the structure of society: "Ignorance of
the fact that man has a wounded nature inclined to evil gives rise to
serious errors in the areas of education, politics, social action and
morals."[85] In the list of areas where the pernicious effects of sin are
evident, the economy has been included for some time now. We
have a clear proof of this at the present time. The conviction that
man is self-sufficient and can successfully eliminate the evil present
in history by his own action alone has led him to confuse happiness
and salvation with immanent forms of material prosperity and social
action. Then, the conviction that the economy must be autonomous,
that it must be shielded from "influences" of a moral character, has
led man to abuse the economic process in a thoroughly destructive
way. In the long term, these convictions have led to economic,
social and political systems that trample upon personal and social
freedom, and are therefore unable to deliver the justice that they
promise. As I said in my Encyclical Letter *Spe Salvi*, history is

---

[85] *Catechism of the Catholic Church*, 407; cf. John Paul II, Encyclical Letter *Centesimus Annus*, 25: *loc. cit.*, 822-824.

143

thereby deprived of *Christian hope*,[86] deprived of a powerful social resource at the service of integral human development, sought in freedom and in justice. Hope encourages reason and gives it the strength to direct the will.[87] It is already present in faith, indeed it is called forth by faith. Charity in truth feeds on hope and, at the same time, manifests it. As the absolutely gratuitous gift of God, hope bursts into our lives as something not due to us, something that transcends every law of justice. Gift by its nature goes beyond merit, its rule is that of superabundance. It takes first place in our souls as a sign of God's presence in us, a sign of what he expects from us. Truth - which is itself gift, in the same way as charity - is greater than we are, as Saint Augustine teaches.[88] Likewise the truth of ourselves, of our personal conscience, is first of all *given* to us. In every cognitive process, truth is not something that we produce, it is always found, or better, received. Truth, like love, "is neither planned nor willed, but somehow imposes itself upon human beings."[89]

Because it is a gift received by everyone, charity in truth is a force that builds community, it brings all people together without imposing barriers or limits. The human community that we build by ourselves can never, purely by its own strength, be a fully fraternal community, nor can it overcome every division and become a truly universal community. The unity of the human race, a fraternal communion transcending every barrier, is called into being by the word of God-who-is-Love. In addressing this key question, we must make it clear, on the one hand, that the logic of gift does

---

87 Cf. *ibid.*, 23: *loc. cit.*, 1004-1005.

88 Saint Augustine expounds this teaching in detail in his dialogue on free will (*De libero arbitrio*, II, 3, 8ff.). He indicates the existence within the human soul of an "internal sense". This sense consists in an act that is fulfilled outside the normal functions of reason, an act that is not the result of reflection, but is almost instinctive, through which reason, realising its transient and fallible nature, admits the existence of something eternal, higher than itself, something absolutely true and certain. The name that Saint Augustine gives to this interior truth is at times the name of God (*Confessions* X, 24, 35; XII, 25, 35; *De libero arbitrio* II, 3, 8), more often that of Christ (*De magistro* 11:38; *Confessions* VII, 18, 24; XI, 2, 4).

89 Benedict XVI, Encyclical Letter *Deus Caritas Est*, 3: *loc. cit.*, 219.

not exclude justice, nor does it merely sit alongside it as a second element added from without; on the other hand, economic, social and political development, if it is to be authentically human, needs to make room for the *principle of gratuitousness* as an expression of fraternity.

35. In a climate of mutual trust, the *market* is the economic institution that permits encounter between persons, inasmuch as they are economic subjects who make use of contracts to regulate their relations as they exchange goods and services of equivalent value between them, in order to satisfy their needs and desires. The market is subject to the principles of so-called *commutative justice*, which regulates the relations of giving and receiving between parties to a transaction. But the social doctrine of the Church has unceasingly highlighted the importance of *distributive justice* and *social justice* for the market economy, not only because it belongs within a broader social and political context, but also because of the wider network of relations within which it operates. In fact, if the market is governed solely by the principle of the equivalence in value of exchanged goods, it cannot produce the social cohesion that it requires in order to function well. *Without internal forms of solidarity and mutual trust, the market cannot completely fulfil its proper economic function.* And today it is this trust which has ceased to exist, and the loss of trust is a grave loss. It was timely when Paul VI in *Populorum Progressio* insisted that the economic system itself would benefit from the wide-ranging practice of justice, inasmuch as the first to gain from the development of poor countries would be rich ones.[90] According to the Pope, it was not just a matter of correcting dysfunctions through assistance. The poor are not to be considered a "burden",[91] but a resource, even from the purely economic point of view. It is nevertheless erroneous to hold that the market economy has an inbuilt need for a quota of poverty and underdevelopment in order to function at its best. It is in the

---

[90] Cf. no. 49: *loc. cit.*, 281.

[91] John Paul II, Encyclical Letter *Centesimus Annus*, 28: *loc. cit.*, 827-828.

interests of the market to promote emancipation, but in order to do so effectively, it cannot rely only on itself, because it is not able to produce by itself something that lies outside its competence. It must draw its moral energies from other subjects that are capable of generating them.

36. Economic activity cannot solve all social problems through the simple application of *commercial logic*. This needs to be *directed towards the pursuit of the common good*, for which the political community in particular must also take responsibility. Therefore, it must be borne in mind that grave imbalances are produced when economic action, conceived merely as an engine for wealth creation, is detached from political action, conceived as a means for pursuing justice through redistribution.

The Church has always held that economic action is not to be regarded as something opposed to society. In and of itself, the market is not, and must not become, the place where the strong subdue the weak. Society does not have to protect itself from the market, as if the development of the latter were *ipso facto* to entail the death of authentically human relations. Admittedly, the market can be a negative force, not because it is so by nature, but because a certain ideology can make it so. It must be remembered that the market does not exist in the pure state. It is shaped by the cultural configurations which define it and give it direction. Economy and finance, as instruments, can be used badly when those at the helm are motivated by purely selfish ends. Instruments that are good in themselves can thereby be transformed into harmful ones. But it is man's darkened reason that produces these consequences, not the instrument *per se*. Therefore it is not the instrument that must be called to account, but individuals, their moral conscience and their personal and social responsibility.

The Church's social doctrine holds that authentically human social relationships of friendship, solidarity and reciprocity can also be conducted within economic activity, and not only outside it or "after" it. The economic sphere is neither ethically neutral, nor inherently inhuman and opposed to society. It is part and parcel of human activity and precisely because it is human, it must be structured and governed in an ethical manner.

The great challenge before us, accentuated by the problems of development in this global era and made even more urgent by the economic and financial crisis, is to demonstrate, in thinking and behaviour, not only that traditional principles of social ethics like transparency, honesty and responsibility cannot be ignored or attenuated, but also that in *commercial relationships* the *principle of gratuitousness* and the logic of gift as an expression of fraternity can and must *find their place within normal economic activity*. This is a human demand at the present time, but it is also demanded by economic logic. It is a demand both of charity and of truth.

37. The Church's social doctrine has always maintained that *justice must be applied to every phase of economic activity*, because this is always concerned with man and his needs. Locating resources, financing, production, consumption and all the other phases in the economic cycle inevitably have moral implications. *Thus every economic decision has a moral consequence.* The social sciences and the direction taken by the contemporary economy point to the same conclusion. Perhaps at one time it was conceivable that first the creation of wealth could be entrusted to the economy, and then the task of distributing it could be assigned to politics. Today that would be more difficult, given that economic activity is no longer circumscribed within territorial limits, while the authority of governments continues to be principally local. Hence the canons of justice must be respected from the outset, as the economic process unfolds, and not just afterwards or incidentally. Space also needs to be created within the market for economic activity carried out by subjects who freely choose to act according to principles other than those of pure profit, without sacrificing the production of economic value in the process. The many economic entities that draw their origin from religious and lay initiatives demonstrate that this is concretely possible.

In the global era, the economy is influenced by competitive models tied to cultures that differ greatly among themselves. The different forms of economic enterprise to which they give rise find their main point of encounter in commutative justice. *Economic life* undoubtedly requires *contracts*, in order to regulate relations of exchange between goods of equivalent value. But it also needs *just laws* and *forms of redistribution* governed by politics, and what is more, it needs works redolent of the *spirit of gift*. The economy in the global era seems to privilege the former logic, that of contractual exchange, but directly or indirectly it also demonstrates its need for the other two: political logic, and the logic of the unconditional gift.

38. My predecessor John Paul II drew attention to this question in *Centesimus Annus,* when he spoke of the need for a system with three subjects: the *market*, the *State* and *civil society*.[92] He saw civil society as the most natural setting for an *economy of gratuitousness* and fraternity, but did not mean to deny it a place in the other two settings. Today we can say that economic life must be understood as a multi-layered phenomenon: in every one of these layers, to varying degrees and in ways specifically suited to each, the aspect of fraternal reciprocity must be present. In the global era, economic activity cannot prescind from gratuitousness, which fosters and disseminates solidarity and responsibility for justice and the common good among the different economic players. It is clearly a specific and profound form of economic democracy. Solidarity is first and foremost a sense of responsibility on the part of everyone with regard to everyone,[93] and it cannot therefore be merely delegated to the State. While in the past it was possible to argue that justice had to come first and gratuitousness could follow afterwards, as a complement, today it is clear that without gratuitousness, there can be no justice in the first place. What is needed, therefore, is a market that permits the free operation, in conditions of equal opportunity, of enterprises in pursuit of different institutional ends. Alongside profit-oriented private enterprise and the various types of public enterprise, there must

---

[92] Cf. no. 35: *loc. cit.*, 836-838.

[93] Cf. John Paul II, Encyclical Letter *Sollicitudo Rei Socialis*, 38: *loc. cit.*, 565-566.

be room for commercial entities based on mutualist principles and pursuing social ends to take root and express themselves. It is from their reciprocal encounter in the marketplace that one may expect hybrid forms of commercial behaviour to emerge, and hence an attentiveness to ways of *civilizing the economy*. Charity in truth, in this case, requires that shape and structure be given to those types of economic initiative which, without rejecting profit, aim at a higher goal than the mere logic of the exchange of equivalents, of profit as an end in itself.

39. Paul VI in *Populorum Progressio* called for the creation of *a model of market economy capable of including within its range all peoples and not just the better off*. He called for efforts to build a more human world for all, a world in which "all will be able to give and receive, without one group making progress at the expense of the other."[94] In this way he was applying on a global scale the insights and aspirations contained in *Rerum Novarum*, written when, as a result of the Industrial Revolution, the idea was first proposed - somewhat ahead of its time - that the civil order, for its self-regulation, also needed intervention from the State for purposes of redistribution. Not only is this vision threatened today by the way in which markets and societies are opening up, but it is evidently insufficient to satisfy the demands of a fully humane economy. What the Church's social doctrine has always sustained, on the basis of its vision of man and society, is corroborated today by the dynamics of globalisation.

When both the logic of the market and the logic of the State come to an agreement that each will continue to exercise a monopoly over its respective area of influence, in the long term much is lost: solidarity in relations between citizens, participation and adherence, actions of gratuitousness, all of which stand in contrast with *giving in order to acquire* (the logic of exchange) and *giving through duty* (the logic of public obligation, imposed by State law). In order to defeat underdevelopment, action is required not only

---

[94] No. 44: *loc. cit.*, 279.

on improving exchange-based transactions and implanting public welfare structures, but above all on gradually *increasing openness, in a world context, to forms of economic activity marked by quotas of gratuitousness and communion* The exclusively binary model of market-plus-State is corrosive of society, while economic forms based on solidarity, which find their natural home in civil society without being restricted to it, build up society. The market of gratuitousness does not exist, and attitudes of gratuitousness cannot be established by law. Yet both the market and politics need individuals who are open to reciprocal gift.

40. Today's international economic scene, marked by grave deviations and failures, requires a *profoundly new way of understanding business enterprise*. Old models are disappearing, but promising new ones are taking shape on the horizon. Without doubt, one of the greatest risks for businesses is that they are almost exclusively answerable to their investors, thereby limiting their social value. Owing to their growth in scale and the need for more and more capital, it is becoming increasingly rare for business enterprises to be in the hands of a stable director who feels responsible in the long term, not just the short term, for the life and the results of his company, and it is becoming increasingly rare for businesses to depend on a single territory. Moreover, the so-called outsourcing of production can weaken the company's sense of responsibility towards the stakeholders - namely the workers, the suppliers, the consumers, the natural environment and broader society - in favour of the shareholders, who are not tied to a specific geographical area and who therefore enjoy extraordinary mobility. Today's international capital market offers great freedom of action. Yet there is also increasing awareness of the need for greater *social responsibility* on the part of business. Even if the ethical considerations that currently inform debate on the social responsibility of the corporate world are not all acceptable from the perspective of the Church's social doctrine, there is nevertheless a growing conviction that *business management cannot concern itself only with the interests of the proprietors, but must also assume*

responsibility for all the other stakeholders who contribute to the life of the business: the workers, the clients, the suppliers of various elements of production, the community of reference. In recent years a new cosmopolitan class of *managers* has emerged, who are often answerable only to the shareholders generally consisting of anonymous funds which *de facto* determine their remuneration. By contrast, though, many far-sighted managers today are becoming increasingly aware of the profound links between their enterprise and the territory or territories in which it operates. Paul VI invited people to give serious attention to the damage that can be caused to one's home country by the transfer abroad of capital purely for personal advantage.[95] John Paul II taught that *investment always has moral, as well as economic significance.*[96] All this - it should be stressed - is still valid today, despite the fact that the capital market has been significantly liberalised, and modern technological thinking can suggest that investment is merely a technical act, not a human and ethical one. There is no reason to deny that a certain amount of capital can do good, if invested abroad rather than at home. Yet the requirements of justice must be safeguarded, with due consideration for the way in which the capital was generated and the harm to individuals that will result if it is not used where it was produced.[97] What should be avoided is a speculative *use of financial resources* that yields to the temptation of seeking only short-term profit, without regard for the long-term sustainability of the enterprise, its benefit to the real economy and attention to the advancement, in suitable and appropriate ways, of further economic initiatives in countries in need of development. It is true that the export of investments and skills can benefit the populations of the receiving country. Labour and technical knowledge are a universal good. Yet it is not right to export these things merely for the sake of obtaining advantageous conditions, or worse, for purposes of exploitation, without making a real contribution to local society by

---

[95] Cf. *ibid.*, 24: *loc. cit.*, 269.

[96] Cf. Encyclical Letter *Centesimus Annus*, 36: *loc. cit.*, 838-840.

[97] Cf. Paul VI, Encyclical Letter *Populorum Progressio*, 24: *loc. cit.*, 269.

helping to bring about a robust productive and social system, an essential factor for stable development.

41. In the context of this discussion, it is helpful to observe that *business enterprise* involves a *wide range of values*, becoming wider all the time. The continuing hegemony of the binary model of market-plus-State has accustomed us to think only in terms of the private business leader of a capitalistic bent on the one hand, and the State director on the other. In reality, business has to be understood in an articulated way. There are a number of reasons, of a meta-economic kind, for saying this. Business activity has a human significance, prior to its professional one.[98] It is present in all work, understood as a personal action, an *"actus personae"*,[99] which is why every worker should have the chance to make his contribution knowing that in some way "he is working 'for himself'."[100] With good reason, Paul VI taught that "everyone who works is a creator."[101] It is in response to the needs and the dignity of the worker, as well as the needs of society, that there exist various types of business enterprise, over and above the simple distinction between "private" and "public". Each of them requires and expresses a specific business capacity. In order to construct an economy that will soon be in a position to serve the national and global common good, it is appropriate to take account of this broader significance of business activity. It favours cross-fertilisation between different types of business activity, with shifting of competencies from the "non-profit" world to the "profit" world and vice versa, from the public world to that of civil society, from advanced economies to developing countries.

"Political authority" also involves a *wide range of values*, which must not be overlooked in the process of constructing a new order of economic productivity, socially responsible and human in scale.

---

[98] Cf. John Paul II, Encyclical Letter *Centesimus Annus*, 32: *loc. cit.*, 832-833; Paul VI, Encyclical Letter *Populorum Progressio*, 25: *loc. cit.*, 269-270.

[99] John Paul II, Encyclical Letter *Laborem Exercens*, 24: *loc. cit.*, 637-638.

[100] *Ibid.*, 15: *loc. cit.*, 616-618.

[101] Encyclical Letter *Populorum Progressio*, 27: *loc. cit.*, 271.

As well as cultivating differentiated forms of business activity on the global plane, we must also promote a dispersed political authority, effective on different levels. The integrated economy of the present day does not make the role of States redundant, but rather it commits governments to greater collaboration with one another. Both wisdom and prudence suggest not being too precipitous in declaring the demise of the State. In terms of the resolution of the current crisis, the State's role seems destined to grow, as it regains many of its competencies. In some nations, moreover, the construction or reconstruction of the State remains a key factor in their development. The focus of *international aid*, within a solidarity-based plan to resolve today's economic problems, should rather be on consolidating constitutional, juridical and administrative systems in countries that do not yet fully enjoy these goods. Alongside economic aid, there needs to be aid directed towards reinforcing the guarantees proper to the *State of law*: a system of public order and effective imprisonment that respects human rights, truly democratic institutions. The State does not need to have identical characteristics everywhere: the support aimed at strengthening weak constitutional systems can easily be accompanied by the development of other political players, of a cultural, social, territorial or religious nature, alongside the State. The articulation of political authority at the local, national and international levels is one of the best ways of giving direction to the process of economic globalisation. It is also the way to ensure that it does not actually undermine the foundations of democracy.

42. Sometimes *globalisation* is viewed in fatalistic terms, as if the dynamics involved were the product of anonymous impersonal forces or structures independent of the human will.[102] In this regard it is useful to remember that while globalisation should certainly be understood as a socio-economic process, this is not its only dimension. Underneath the more visible process, humanity itself is

---

[102] Cf. Congregation for the Doctrine of the Faith, Instruction on Christian Freedom and Liberation *Libertatis Conscientia* (22nd March 1987), 74: *AAS* 79 (1987), 587.

becoming increasingly interconnected; it is made up of individuals and peoples to whom this process should offer benefits and development,[103] as they assume their respective responsibilities, singly and collectively. The breaking-down of borders is not simply a material fact: it is also a cultural event both in its causes and its effects. If globalisation is viewed from a deterministic standpoint, the criteria with which to evaluate and direct it are lost. As a human reality, it is the product of diverse cultural tendencies, which need to be subjected to a process of discernment. The truth of globalisation as a process and its fundamental ethical criterion are given by the unity of the human family and its development towards what is good. Hence a sustained commitment is needed so as to *promote a person-based and community-oriented cultural process of world-wide integration that is open to transcendence.*

Despite some of its structural elements, which should neither be denied nor exaggerated, "globalisation, *a priori*, is neither good nor bad. It will be what people make of it."[104] We should not be its victims, but rather its protagonists, acting in the light of reason, guided by charity and truth. Blind opposition would be a mistaken and prejudiced attitude, incapable of recognising the positive aspects of the process, with the consequent risk of missing the chance to take advantage of its many opportunities for development. The processes of globalisation, suitably understood and directed, open up the unprecedented possibility of large-scale redistribution of wealth on a world-wide scale; if badly directed, however, they can lead to an increase in poverty and inequality, and could even trigger a global crisis. It is necessary to *correct the malfunctions*, some of them serious, that cause new divisions between peoples and within peoples, and also to ensure that the redistribution of wealth does not come about through the redistribution or increase of poverty: a real danger if the present situation were to be badly managed. For a long time it was thought that poor peoples should

---

[103] Cf. John Paul II, Interview published in the Catholic daily newspaper *La Croix*, 20th August 1997.

[104] John Paul II, *Address to the Pontifical Academy of Social Sciences*, 27th April 2001.

remain at a fixed stage of development, and should be content to receive assistance from the philanthropy of developed peoples. Paul VI strongly opposed this mentality in *Populorum Progressio*. Today the material resources available for rescuing these peoples from poverty are potentially greater than before, but they have ended up largely in the hands of people from developed countries, who have benefited more from the liberalisation that has occurred in the mobility of capital and labour. The world-wide diffusion of forms of prosperity should not therefore be held up by projects that are self-centred, protectionist or at the service of private interests. Indeed the involvement of emerging or developing countries allows us to manage the crisis better today. The transition inherent in the process of globalisation presents great difficulties and dangers that can only be overcome if we are able to appropriate the underlying anthropological and ethical spirit that drives globalisation towards the humanising goal of solidarity. Unfortunately this spirit is often overwhelmed or suppressed by ethical and cultural considerations of an individualistic and utilitarian nature. Globalisation is a multifaceted and complex phenomenon which must be grasped in the diversity and unity of all its different dimensions, including the theological dimension. In this way it will be possible to experience and to *steer the globalisation of humanity in relational terms, in terms of communion and the sharing of goods.*

CHAPTER FOUR

THE DEVELOPMENT OF PEOPLE - RIGHTS AND DUTIES - THE ENVIRONMENT

43. "The reality of human solidarity, which is a benefit for us, also imposes a duty."[105] Many people today would claim that they owe nothing to anyone, except to themselves. They are concerned only with their rights, and they often have great difficulty in taking responsibility for their own and other people's integral development. Hence it is important to call for a renewed reflection on how *rights presuppose duties, if they are not to become mere licence.*[106] Nowadays we are witnessing a grave inconsistency. On the one hand, appeals are made to alleged rights, arbitrary and non-essential in nature, accompanied by the demand that they be recognised and promoted by public structures, while, on the other hand, elementary and basic rights remain unacknowledged and are violated in much of the world.[107] A link has often been noted between claims to a "right to excess", and even to transgression and vice, within affluent societies, and the lack of food, drinkable water, basic instruction and elementary health care in areas of the underdeveloped world and on the outskirts of large metropolitan centres. The link consists in this: individual rights, when detached from a framework of duties which grants them their full meaning, can run wild, leading to an escalation of demands which is effectively unlimited and indiscriminate. An overemphasis on rights leads to a disregard for duties. Duties set a limit on rights because they point to the anthropological and ethical framework of which rights are a part, in this way ensuring that they do not become licence. Duties thereby reinforce rights and call for their defence and promotion as a task to be undertaken in the service of the common good.

---

[105] Paul VI, Encyclical Letter *Populorum Progressio*, 17: *loc. cit.*, 265-266.

[106] Cf. John Paul II, *Message for the 2003 World Day of Peace*, 5: *AAS* 95 (2003), 343.

[107] Cf. *ibid.*

Otherwise, if the only basis of human rights is to be found in the deliberations of an assembly of citizens, those rights can be changed at any time, and so the duty to respect and pursue them fades from the common consciousness. Governments and international bodies can then lose sight of the objectivity and "inviolability" of rights. When this happens, the authentic development of peoples is endangered.[108] Such a way of thinking and acting compromises the authority of international bodies, especially in the eyes of those countries most in need of development. Indeed, the latter demand that the international community take up the duty of helping them to be "artisans of their own destiny",[109] that is, to take up duties of their own. *The sharing of reciprocal duties is a more powerful incentive to action than the mere assertion of rights.*

44. The notion of rights and duties in development must also take account of the problems associated with *population growth*. This is a very important aspect of authentic development, since it concerns the inalienable values of life and the family.[110] To consider population increase as the primary cause of underdevelopment is mistaken, even from an economic point of view. Suffice it to consider, on the one hand, the significant reduction in infant mortality and the rise in average life expectancy found in economically developed countries, and on the other hand, the signs of crisis observable in societies that are registering an alarming decline in their birth rate. Due attention must obviously be given to responsible procreation, which among other things has a positive contribution to make to integral human development. The Church, in her concern for man's authentic development, urges him to have full respect for human values in the exercise of his sexuality. It cannot be reduced merely to pleasure or entertainment, nor can sex education be reduced to technical instruction aimed solely at protecting the interested parties from possible disease or the "risk" of procreation. This would be to

[108] Cf. Benedict XVI, *Message for the 2007 World Day of Peace*, 13: *loc. cit.*, 781-782.
[109] Paul VI, Encyclical Letter *Populorum Progressio*, 65: *loc. cit.*, 289.
[110] Cf. *ibid.*, 36-37: *loc. cit.*, 275-276.

impoverish and disregard the deeper meaning of sexuality, a meaning which needs to be acknowledged and responsibly appropriated not only by individuals but also by the community. It is irresponsible to view sexuality merely as a source of pleasure, and likewise to regulate it through strategies of mandatory birth control. In either case materialistic ideas and policies are at work, and individuals are ultimately subjected to various forms of violence. Against such policies, there is a need to defend the primary competence of the family in the area of sexuality,[111] as opposed to the State and its restrictive policies, and to ensure that parents are suitably prepared to undertake their responsibilities.

Morally responsible openness to life represents a rich social and economic resource. Populous nations have been able to emerge from poverty thanks not least to the size of their population and the talents of their people. On the other hand, formerly prosperous nations are presently passing through a phase of uncertainty and in some cases decline, precisely because of their falling birth rates; this has become a crucial problem for highly affluent societies. The decline in births, falling at times beneath the so-called "replacement level", also puts a strain on social welfare systems, increases their cost, eats into savings and hence the financial resources needed for investment, reduces the availability of qualified labourers, and narrows the "brain pool" upon which nations can draw for their needs. Furthermore, smaller and at times miniscule families run the risk of impoverishing social relations, and failing to ensure effective forms of solidarity. These situations are symptomatic of scant confidence in the future and moral weariness. It is thus becoming a social and even economic necessity once more to hold up to future generations the beauty of marriage and the family, and the fact that these institutions correspond to the deepest needs and dignity of the person. In view of this, States are called to *enact policies promoting the centrality and the integrity of the family* founded on marriage between a man and a woman, the primary vital cell of

---

[111] Cf. *ibid.*, 37: *loc. cit.*, 275-276.

society,[112] and to assume responsibility for its economic and fiscal needs, while respecting its essentially relational character.

45. Striving to meet the deepest moral needs of the person also has important and beneficial repercussions at the level of economics. *The economy needs ethics in order to function correctly* - not any ethics whatsoever, but an ethics which is people-centred. Today we hear much talk of ethics in the world of economy, finance and business. Research centres and seminars in business ethics are on the rise; the system of ethical certification is spreading throughout the developed world as part of the movement of ideas associated with the responsibilities of business towards society. Banks are proposing "ethical" accounts and investment funds. "Ethical financing" is being developed, especially through micro-credit and, more generally, micro-finance. These processes are praiseworthy and deserve much support. Their positive effects are also being felt in the less developed areas of the world. It would be advisable, however, to develop a sound criterion of discernment, since the adjective "ethical" can be abused. When the word is used generically, it can lend itself to any number of interpretations, even to the point where it includes decisions and choices contrary to justice and authentic human welfare.

Much in fact depends on the underlying system of morality. On this subject the Church's social doctrine can make a specific contribution, since it is based on man's creation "in the image of God" (*Gn* 1:27), a datum which gives rise to the inviolable dignity of the human person and the transcendent value of natural moral norms. When business ethics prescinds from these two pillars, it inevitably risks losing its distinctive nature and it falls prey to forms of exploitation; more specifically, it risks becoming subservient to existing economic and financial systems rather than correcting their dysfunctional aspects. Among other things, it risks being used to justify the financing of projects that are in

---

[112] Cf. Second Vatican Ecumenical Council, Decree on the Apostolate of Lay People *Apostolicam Actuositatem*, 11.

reality unethical. The word "ethical", then, should not be used to make ideological distinctions, as if to suggest that initiatives not formally so designated would not be ethical. Efforts are needed - and it is essential to say this - not only to create "ethical" sectors or segments of the economy or the world of finance, but to ensure that the whole economy - the whole of finance - is ethical, not merely by virtue of an external label, but by its respect for requirements intrinsic to its very nature. The Church's social teaching is quite clear on the subject, recalling that the economy, in all its branches, constitutes a sector of human activity.[113]

46. When we consider the issues involved in the *relationship between business and ethics*, as well as the evolution currently taking place in methods of production, it would appear that the traditionally valid distinction between profit-based companies and non-profit organisations can no longer do full justice to reality, or offer practical direction for the future. In recent decades a broad intermediate area has emerged between the two types of enterprise. It is made up of traditional companies which nonetheless subscribe to social aid agreements in support of underdeveloped countries, charitable foundations associated with individual companies, groups of companies oriented towards social welfare, and the diversified world of the so-called "civil economy" and the "economy of communion". This is not merely a matter of a "third sector", but of a broad new composite reality embracing the private and public spheres, one which does not exclude profit, but instead considers it a means for achieving human and social ends. Whether such companies distribute dividends or not, whether their juridical structure corresponds to one or other of the established forms, becomes secondary in relation to their willingness to view profit as a means of achieving the goal of a more humane market and society. It is to be hoped that these new kinds of enterprise will succeed in finding a suitable juridical and fiscal structure in every

---

[113] Cf. Paul VI, Encyclical Letter *Populorum Progressio*, 14: *loc. cit.*, 264; John Paul II, Encyclical Letter *Centesimus Annus*, 32: *loc. cit.*, 832-833.

country. Without prejudice to the importance and the economic and
social benefits of the more traditional forms of business, they steer
the system towards a clearer and more complete assumption of
duties on the part of economic subjects. And not only that. *The very
plurality of institutional forms of business gives rise to a market
which is not only more civilized but also more competitive.*

47. The strengthening of different types of businesses, especially
those capable of viewing profit as a means for achieving the goal
of a more humane market and society, must also be pursued in
those countries that are excluded or marginalised from the
influential circles of the global economy. In these countries it is
very important to move ahead with projects based on subsidiarity,
suitably planned and managed, aimed at affirming rights yet also
providing for the assumption of corresponding responsibilities.
In *development programmes*, the principle of the *centrality
of the human person*, as the subject primarily responsible for
development, must be preserved. The principal concern must be to
improve the actual living conditions of the people in a given region,
thus enabling them to carry out those duties which their poverty
does not presently allow them to fulfil. Social concern must never
be an abstract attitude. Development programmes, if they are to
be adapted to individual situations, need to be flexible; and the
people who benefit from them ought to be directly involved in their
planning and implementation. The criteria to be applied should
aspire towards incremental development in a context of solidarity
- with careful monitoring of results - inasmuch as there are no
universally valid solutions. Much depends on the way programmes
are managed in practice. "The peoples themselves have the prime
responsibility to work for their own development. But they will
not bring this about in isolation."[114] These words of Paul VI are all
the more timely nowadays, as our world becomes progressively
more integrated. The dynamics of inclusion are hardly automatic.
Solutions need to be carefully designed to correspond to people's

---

[114] Paul VI, Encyclical Letter *Populorum Progressio*, 77: *loc. cit.*, 295.

concrete lives, based on a prudential evaluation of each situation. Alongside macro-projects, there is a place for micro-projects, and above all there is need for the active mobilisation of all the subjects of civil society, both juridical and physical persons.

International cooperation requires people who can be part of the process of economic and human development through the solidarity of their presence, supervision, training and respect. From this standpoint, international organisations might question the actual effectiveness of their bureaucratic and administrative machinery, which is often excessively costly. At times it happens that those who receive aid become subordinate to the aid-givers, and the poor serve to perpetuate expensive bureaucracies which consume an excessively high percentage of funds intended for development. Hence it is to be hoped that all international agencies and non-governmental organisations will commit themselves to complete transparency, informing donors and the public of the percentage of their income allocated to programmes of cooperation, the actual content of those programmes and, finally, the detailed expenditure of the institution itself.

48. Today the subject of development is also closely related to the duties arising from *our relationship to the natural environment*. The environment is God's gift to everyone, and in our use of it we have a responsibility towards the poor, towards future generations and towards humanity as a whole. When nature, including the human being, is viewed as the result of mere chance or evolutionary determinism, our sense of responsibility wanes. In nature, the believer recognises the wonderful result of God's creative activity, which we may use responsibly to satisfy our legitimate needs, material or otherwise, while respecting the intrinsic balance of creation. If this vision is lost, we end up either considering nature an untouchable taboo or, on the contrary, abusing it. Neither attitude is consonant with the Christian vision of nature as the fruit of God's creation.

Nature expresses a design of love and truth. It is prior to us, and it has been given to us by God as the setting for our life. Nature speaks to us of the Creator (cf. *Rm* 1:20) and his love for humanity. It is destined to be "recapitulated" in Christ at the end of time (cf. *Ep* 1:9-10; *Col* 1:19-20). Thus it too is a "vocation".[115] Nature is at our disposal not as "a heap of scattered refuse",[116] but as a gift of the Creator who has given it an inbuilt order, enabling man to draw from it the principles needed in order "to till it and keep it" (*Gn* 2:15). But it should also be stressed that it is contrary to authentic development to view nature as something more important than the human person. This position leads to attitudes of neo-paganism or a new pantheism - human salvation cannot come from nature alone, understood in a purely naturalistic sense. This having been said, it is also necessary to reject the opposite position, which aims at total technical dominion over nature, because the natural environment is more than raw material to be manipulated at our pleasure; it is a wondrous work of the Creator containing a "grammar" which sets forth ends and criteria for its wise use, not its reckless exploitation. Today much harm is done to development precisely as a result of these distorted notions. Reducing nature merely to a collection of contingent data ends up doing violence to the environment and even encouraging activity that fails to respect human nature itself. Our nature, constituted not only by matter but also by spirit, and as such, endowed with transcendent meaning and aspirations, is also normative for culture. Human beings interpret and shape the natural environment through culture, which in turn is given direction by the responsible use of freedom, in accordance with the dictates of the moral law. Consequently, projects for integral human development cannot ignore coming generations, but need to be marked by solidarity and *inter-generational justice*, while taking into account a variety of contexts: ecological, juridical, economic, political and cultural.[117]

---

[115] John Paul II, *Message for the 1990 World Day of Peace*, 6: *AAS* 82 (1990), 150.

[116] Heraclitus of Ephesus (Ephesus, c. 535 B.C. - c. 475 B.C.), Fragment 22B124, in H. Diels and W. Kranz, *Die Fragmente der Vorsokratiker*, Weidmann, Berlin, 1952, 6th ed.

[117] Pontifical Council for Justice And Peace, *Compendium of the Social Doctrine of the Church*, 451-487.

49. Questions linked to the care and preservation of the environment today need to give due consideration to *the energy problem*. The fact that some States, power groups and companies hoard non-renewable energy resources represents a grave obstacle to development in poor countries. Those countries lack the economic means either to gain access to existing sources of non-renewable energy or to finance research into new alternatives. The stockpiling of natural resources, which in many cases are found in the poor countries themselves, gives rise to exploitation and frequent conflicts between and within nations. These conflicts are often fought on the soil of those same countries, with a heavy toll of death, destruction and further decay. The international community has an urgent duty to find institutional means of regulating the exploitation of non-renewable resources, involving poor countries in the process, in order to plan together for the future.

On this front too, there is a *pressing moral need for renewed solidarity*, especially in relationships between developing countries and those that are highly industrialised.[118] The technologically advanced societies can and must lower their domestic energy consumption, either through an evolution in manufacturing methods or through greater ecological sensitivity among their citizens. It should be added that at present it is possible to achieve improved energy efficiency while at the same time encouraging research into alternative forms of energy. What is also needed, though, is a worldwide redistribution of energy resources, so that countries lacking those resources can have access to them. The fate of those countries cannot be left in the hands of whoever is first to claim the spoils, or whoever is able to prevail over the rest. Here we are dealing with major issues; if they are to be faced adequately, then everyone must responsibly recognise the impact they will have on future generations, particularly on the many young people in the poorer nations, who "ask to assume their active part in the construction of a better world".[119]

---

[118] Cf. John Paul II, *Message for the 1990 World Day of Peace*, 10: *loc. cit.*, 152-153.

[119] Paul VI, Encyclical Letter *Populorum Progressio*, 65: *loc. cit.*, 289.

50. This responsibility is a global one, for it is concerned not just with energy but with the whole of creation, which must not be bequeathed to future generations depleted of its resources. Human beings legitimately exercise a *responsible stewardship over nature*, in order to protect it, to enjoy its fruits and to cultivate it in new ways, with the assistance of advanced technologies, so that it can worthily accommodate and feed the world's population. On this earth there is room for everyone: here the entire human family must find the resources to live with dignity, through the help of nature itself - God's gift to his children - and through hard work and creativity. At the same time we must recognise our grave duty to hand the earth on to future generations in such a condition that they too can worthily inhabit it and continue to cultivate it. This means being committed to making joint decisions "after pondering responsibly the road to be taken, decisions aimed at strengthening that *covenant between human beings and the environment*, which should mirror the creative love of God, from whom we come and towards whom we are journeying."[120] Let us hope that the international community and individual governments will succeed in countering harmful ways of treating the environment. It is likewise incumbent upon the competent authorities to make every effort to ensure that the economic and social costs of using up shared environmental resources are recognised with transparency and fully borne by those who incur them, not by other peoples or future generations: the protection of the environment, of resources and of the climate obliges all international leaders to act jointly and to show a readiness to work in good faith, respecting the law and promoting solidarity with the weakest regions of the planet.[121] One of the greatest challenges facing the economy is to achieve the most efficient use - not abuse - of natural resources, based on a realisation that the notion of "efficiency" is not value-free.

---

[120] Benedict XVI, *Message for the 2008 World Day of Peace*, 7: AAS 100 (2008), 41.

[121] Cf. Benedict XVI, *Address to the General Assembly of the United Nations Organisation*, New York, 18th April 2008.

51. *The way humanity treats the environment influences the way it treats itself, and vice versa.* This invites contemporary society to a serious review of its life-style, which, in many parts of the world, is prone to hedonism and consumerism, regardless of their harmful consequences.[122] What is needed is an effective shift in mentality which can lead to the adoption of *new life-styles* "in which the quest for truth, beauty, goodness and communion with others for the sake of common growth are the factors which determine consumer choices, savings and investments."[123] Every violation of solidarity and civic friendship harms the environment, just as environmental deterioration in turn upsets relations in society. Nature, especially in our time, is so integrated into the dynamics of society and culture that by now it hardly constitutes an independent variable. Desertification and the decline in productivity in some agricultural areas are also the result of impoverishment and underdevelopment among their inhabitants. When incentives are offered for their economic and cultural development, nature itself is protected. Moreover, how many natural resources are squandered by wars! Peace in and among peoples would also provide greater protection for nature. The hoarding of resources, especially water, can generate serious conflicts among the peoples involved. Peaceful agreement about the use of resources can protect nature and, at the same time, the well-being of the societies concerned.

The Church has a responsibility towards creation and she must assert this responsibility in the public sphere. In so doing, she must defend not only earth, water and air as gifts of creation that belong to everyone. She must above all protect mankind from self-destruction. There is need for what might be called a human ecology, correctly understood. The deterioration of nature is in fact closely connected to the culture that shapes human coexistence: *when "human ecology"*[124] *is respected within society, environmental ecology also benefits.* Just as human virtues are interrelated, such

---

[122] Cf. John Paul II, *Message for the 1990 World Day of Peace*, 13: *loc. cit.,* 154-155.

[123] John Paul II, Encyclical Letter *Centesimus Annus*, 36: *loc. cit.,* 838-840.

[124] *Ibid.*, 38: *loc. cit.,* 840-841; Benedict XVI, *Message for the 2007 World Day of Peace*, 8: *loc. cit.,* 779.

that the weakening of one places others at risk, so the ecological system is based on respect for a plan that affects both the health of society and its good relationship with nature.

In order to protect nature, it is not enough to intervene with economic incentives or deterrents; not even an apposite education is sufficient. These are important steps, but *the decisive issue is the overall moral tenor of society*. If there is a lack of respect for the right to life and to a natural death, if human conception, gestation and birth are made artificial, if human embryos are sacrificed to research, the conscience of society ends up losing the concept of human ecology and, along with it, that of environmental ecology. It is contradictory to insist that future generations respect the natural environment when our educational systems and laws do not help them to respect themselves. The book of nature is one and indivisible: it takes in not only the environment but also life, sexuality, marriage, the family, social relations: in a word, integral human development. Our duties towards the environment are linked to our duties towards the human person, considered in himself and in relation to others. It would be wrong to uphold one set of duties while trampling on the other. Herein lies a grave contradiction in our mentality and practice today: one which demeans the person, disrupts the environment and damages society.

52. Truth, and the love which it reveals, cannot be produced: they can only be received as a gift. Their ultimate source is not, and cannot be, mankind, but only God, who is himself Truth and Love. This principle is extremely important for society and for development, since neither can be a purely human product; the vocation to development on the part of individuals and peoples is not based simply on human choice, but is an intrinsic part of a plan that is prior to us and constitutes for all of us a duty to be freely accepted. That which is prior to us and constitutes us - subsistent Love and Truth - shows us what goodness is, and in what our true happiness consists. *It shows us the road to true development.*

CHAPTER FIVE

THE COOPERATION OF THE HUMAN FAMILY

53. One of the deepest forms of poverty a person can experience is isolation. If we look closely at other kinds of poverty, including material forms, we see that they are born from isolation, from not being loved or from difficulties in being able to love. Poverty is often produced by a rejection of God's love, by man's basic and tragic tendency to close in on himself, thinking himself to be self-sufficient or merely an insignificant and ephemeral fact, a "stranger" in a random universe. Man is alienated when he is alone, when he is detached from reality, when he stops thinking and believing in a foundation.[125] All of humanity is alienated when too much trust is placed in merely human projects, ideologies and false utopias.[126] Today humanity appears much more interactive than in the past: this shared sense of being close to one another must be transformed into true communion. *The development of peoples depends, above all, on a recognition that the human race is a single family* working together in true communion, not simply a group of subjects who happen to live side by side.[127]

Pope Paul VI noted that "the world is in trouble because of the lack of thinking".[128] He was making an observation, but also expressing a wish: a new trajectory of thinking is needed in order to arrive at a better understanding of the implications of our being one family; interaction among the peoples of the world calls us to embark upon this new trajectory, so that integration can signify solidarity[129] rather

---

[125] Cf. John Paul II, Encyclical Letter *Centesimus Annus*, 41: *loc. cit.*, 843-845.

[126] Cf. *ibid.*

[127] Cf. John Paul II, Encyclical Letter *Evangelium Vitae*, 20: *loc. cit.*, 422-424.

[128] Encyclical Letter *Populorum Progressio*, 85: *loc. cit.*, 298-299.

[129] Cf. John Paul II, *Message for the 1998 World Day of Peace*, 3: *AAS* 90 (1998), 150; *Address to the Members of the Vatican Foundation "Centesimus Annus – Pro Pontifice"*, 9th May 1998, 2; *Address to the Civil Authorities and Diplomatic Corps of Austria*, 20th June 1998, 8; *Message to the Catholic University of the Sacred Heart*, 5th May 2000, 6.

than marginalisation. Thinking of this kind requires a *deeper critical evaluation of the category of relation*. This is a task that cannot be undertaken by the social sciences alone, insofar as the contribution of disciplines such as metaphysics and theology is needed if man's transcendent dignity is to be properly understood.

As a spiritual being, the human creature is defined through interpersonal relations. The more authentically he or she lives these relations, the more his or her own personal identity matures. It is not by isolation that man establishes his worth, but by placing himself in relation with others and with God. Hence these relations take on fundamental importance. The same holds true for peoples as well. A metaphysical understanding of the relations between persons is therefore of great benefit for their development. In this regard, reason finds inspiration and direction in Christian revelation, according to which the human community does not absorb the individual, annihilating his autonomy, as happens in the various forms of totalitarianism, but rather values him all the more because the relation between individual and community is a relation between one totality and another.[130] Just as a family does not submerge the identities of its individual members, just as the Church rejoices in each "new creation" (*Ga* 6:15; *2 Co* 5:17) incorporated by Baptism into her living Body, so too the unity of the human family does not submerge the identities of individuals, peoples and cultures, but makes them more transparent to each other and links them more closely in their legitimate diversity.

54. The theme of development can be identified with the inclusion-in-relation of all individuals and peoples within the one community of the human family, built in solidarity on the basis of the fundamental values of justice and peace. This perspective is illuminated in a striking way by the relationship between the Persons of the Trinity within the one divine Substance. The Trinity is absolute unity insofar as the three divine Persons are pure relationality. The

[130] According to Saint Thomas *"ratio partis contrariatur rationi personae"*, *In III Sent.*, d. 5, q. 3, a. 2; also *"Homo non ordinatur ad communitatem politicam secundum se totum et secundum omnia sua"*, *Summa Theologiae* I-II, q. 21, a. 4, ad 3.

reciprocal transparency among the divine Persons is total and the bond between each of them complete, since they constitute a unique and absolute unity. God desires to incorporate us into this reality of communion as well: "that they may be one even as we are one" (*Jn* 17:22). The Church is a sign and instrument of this unity.[131] Relationships between human beings throughout history cannot but be enriched by reference to this divine model. In particular, *in the light of the revealed mystery of the Trinity*, we understand that true openness does not mean loss of individual identity but profound interpenetration. This also emerges from the common human experiences of love and truth. Just as the sacramental love of spouses unites them spiritually in "one flesh" (*Gn* 2:24; *Mt* 19:5; *Ep* 5:31) and makes out of the two a real and relational unity, so in an analogous way truth unites spirits and causes them to think in unison, attracting them as a unity to itself.

55. The Christian revelation of the unity of the human race presupposes a *metaphysical interpretation of the "humanum" in which relationality is an essential element*. Other cultures and religions teach brotherhood and peace and are therefore of enormous importance to integral human development. Some religious and cultural attitudes, however, do not fully embrace the principle of love and truth and therefore end up retarding or even obstructing authentic human development. There are certain religious cultures in the world today that do not oblige men and women to live in communion but rather cut them off from one other in a search for individual well-being, limited to the gratification of psychological desires. Furthermore, a certain proliferation of different religious "paths", attracting small groups or even single individuals, together with religious syncretism, can give rise to separation and disengagement. One possible negative effect of the process of globalisation is the tendency to favour this kind

---

[131] Cf. Second Vatican Ecumenical Council, Dogmatic Constitution on the Church *Lumen Gentium*, 1.

of syncretism[132] by encouraging forms of "religion" that, instead of bringing people together, alienate them from one another and distance them from reality. At the same time, some religious and cultural traditions persist which ossify society in rigid social groupings, in magical beliefs that fail to respect the dignity of the person, and in attitudes of subjugation to occult powers. In these contexts, love and truth have difficulty asserting themselves, and authentic development is impeded.

For this reason, while it may be true that development needs the religions and cultures of different peoples, it is equally true that adequate discernment is needed. Religious freedom does not mean religious indifferentism, nor does it imply that all religions are equal.[133] Discernment is needed regarding the contribution of cultures and religions, especially on the part of those who wield political power, if the social community is to be built up in a spirit of respect for the common good. Such discernment has to be based on the criterion of charity and truth. Since the development of persons and peoples is at stake, this discernment will have to take account of the need for emancipation and inclusivity, in the context of a truly universal human community. "The whole man and all men" is also the criterion for evaluating cultures and religions. Christianity, the religion of the "God who has a human face",[134] contains this very criterion within itself.

56. The Christian religion and other religions can offer their contribution to development *only if God has a place in the public realm*, specifically in regard to its cultural, social, economic, and particularly its political dimensions. The Church's social doctrine came into being in order to claim "citizenship status" for the

---

[132] Cf. John Paul II, *Address to the Sixth Public Session of the Pontifical Academies of Theology and of Saint Thomas Aquinas*, 8th November 2001, 3.

[133] Cf. Congregation for the Doctrine of the Faith, Declaration on the Unicity and Salvific Universality of Jesus Christ and the Church *Dominus Iesus* (6th August 2000), 22: *AAS* 92 (2000), 763-764; Id., *Doctrinal Note on some questions regarding the participation of Catholics in political life* (24th November 2002), 8: *AAS* 96 (2004), 369-370.

[134] Benedict XVI, Encyclical Letter *Spe Salvi*, 31: *loc. cit.*, 1010; *Address to the Participants in the Fourth National Congress of the Church in Italy*, Verona, 19th October 2006.

Christian religion.[135] Denying the right to profess one's religion in public and the right to bring the truths of faith to bear upon public life has negative consequences for true development. The exclusion of religion from the public square - and, at the other extreme, religious fundamentalism - hinders an encounter between persons and their collaboration for the progress of humanity. Public life is sapped of its motivation and politics takes on a domineering and aggressive character. Human rights risk being ignored either because they are robbed of their transcendent foundation or because personal freedom is not acknowledged. Secularism and fundamentalism exclude the possibility of fruitful dialogue and effective cooperation between reason and religious faith. *Reason always stands in need of being purified by faith*: this also holds true for political reason, which must not consider itself omnipotent. For its part, *religion always needs to be purified by reason* in order to show its authentically human face. Any breach in this dialogue comes only at an enormous price to human development.

57. Fruitful dialogue between faith and reason cannot but render the work of charity more effective within society, and it constitutes the most appropriate framework for promoting *fraternal collaboration between believers and non-believers* in their shared commitment to working for justice and the peace of the human family. In the Pastoral Constitution *Gaudium et Spes,* the Council fathers asserted that "believers and unbelievers agree almost unanimously that all things on earth should be ordered towards man as to their centre and summit."[136] For believers, the world derives neither from blind chance nor from strict necessity, but from God's plan. This is what gives rise to the duty of believers to unite their efforts with those of all men and women of good will, with the followers of other religions and with non-believers, so that this world of ours may effectively correspond to the divine plan: living as a family

---

[135] John Paul II, Encyclical Letter *Centesimus Annus*, 5: *loc. cit.*, 798-800; Benedict XVI, *Address to the Participants in the Fourth National Congress of the Church in Italy,* Verona, 19th October 2006.

[136] No. 12.

under the Creator's watchful eye. A particular manifestation of charity and a guiding criterion for fraternal cooperation between believers and non-believers is undoubtedly the *principle of subsidiarity*,[137] an expression of inalienable human freedom. Subsidiarity is first and foremost a form of assistance to the human person via the autonomy of intermediate bodies. Such assistance is offered when individuals or groups are unable to accomplish something on their own, and it is always designed to achieve their emancipation, because it fosters freedom and participation through assumption of responsibility. Subsidiarity respects personal dignity by recognising in the person a subject who is always capable of giving something to others. By considering reciprocity as the heart of what it is to be a human being, subsidiarity is the most effective antidote against any form of all-encompassing welfare state. It is able to take account both of the manifold articulation of plans - and therefore of the plurality of subjects - as well as the coordination of those plans. Hence the principle of subsidiarity is particularly well-suited to managing globalisation and directing it towards authentic human development. In order not to produce a dangerous universal power of a tyrannical nature, *the governance of globalisation must be marked by subsidiarity*, articulated into several layers and involving different levels that can work together. Globalisation certainly requires authority, insofar as it poses the problem of a global common good that needs to be pursued. This authority, however, must be organised in a subsidiary and stratified way,[138] if it is not to infringe upon freedom and if it is to yield effective results in practice.

58. *The principle of subsidiarity must remain closely linked to the principle of solidarity and vice versa*, since the former without the latter gives way to social privatism, while the latter without the former gives way to paternalist social assistance that is demeaning

---

[137] Cf. Pius XI, Encyclical Letter *Quadragesimo Anno* (15th May 1931): *AAS* 23 (1931), 203; John Paul II, Encyclical Letter *Centesimus Annus*, 48: *loc. cit.*, 852-854; *Catechism of the Catholic Church*, 1883.

[138] Cf. John XXIII, Encyclical Letter *Pacem in Terris*, *loc. cit.*, 274.

to those in need. This general rule must also be taken broadly into consideration when addressing issues concerning *international development aid*. Such aid, whatever the donors' intentions, can sometimes lock people into a state of dependence and even foster situations of localised oppression and exploitation in the receiving country. Economic aid, in order to be true to its purpose, must not pursue secondary objectives. It must be distributed with the involvement not only of the governments of receiving countries, but also local economic agents and the bearers of culture within civil society, including local Churches. Aid programmes must increasingly acquire the characteristics of participation and completion from the grass roots. Indeed, the most valuable resources in countries receiving development aid are human resources: herein lies the real capital that needs to accumulate in order to guarantee a truly autonomous future for the poorest countries. It should also be remembered that, in the economic sphere, the principal form of assistance needed by developing countries is that of allowing and encouraging the gradual penetration of their products into international markets, thus making it possible for these countries to participate fully in international economic life. Too often in the past, aid has served to create only fringe markets for the products of these donor countries. This was often due to a lack of genuine demand for the products in question: it is therefore necessary to help such countries improve their products and adapt them more effectively to existing demand. Furthermore, there are those who fear the effects of competition through the importation of products - normally agricultural products - from economically poor countries. Nevertheless, it should be remembered that for such countries, the possibility of marketing their products is very often what guarantees their survival in both the short and long term. Just and equitable international trade in agricultural goods can be beneficial to everyone, both to suppliers and to customers. For this reason, not only is commercial orientation needed for production of this kind, but also the establishment of international trade regulations to support it and stronger financing for development in order to increase the productivity of these economies.

59. *Cooperation for development* must not be concerned exclusively with the economic dimension: it offers a wonderful *opportunity for encounter between cultures and peoples.* If the parties to cooperation on the side of economically developed countries - as occasionally happens - fail to take account of their own or others' cultural identity, or the human values that shape it, they cannot enter into meaningful dialogue with the citizens of poor countries. If the latter, in their turn, are uncritically and indiscriminately open to every cultural proposal, they will not be in a position to assume responsibility for their own authentic development.[139] Technologically advanced societies must not confuse their own technological development with a presumed cultural superiority, but must rather rediscover within themselves the oft-forgotten virtues which made it possible for them to flourish throughout their history. Evolving societies must remain faithful to all that is truly human in their traditions, avoiding the temptation to overlay them automatically with the mechanisms of a globalised technological civilisation. In all cultures there are examples of ethical convergence, some isolated, some interrelated, as an expression of the one human nature, willed by the Creator; the tradition of ethical wisdom knows this as the natural law.[140] This universal moral law provides a sound basis for all cultural, religious and political dialogue, and it ensures that the multi-faceted pluralism of cultural diversity does not detach itself from the common quest for truth, goodness and God. Thus adherence to the law etched on human hearts is the precondition for all constructive social cooperation. Every culture has burdens from which it must be freed and shadows from which it must emerge. The Christian faith, by becoming incarnate in cultures and at the same time transcending them, can help them grow in universal brotherhood and solidarity, for the advancement of global and community development.

---

[139] Cf. Paul VI, Encyclical Letter *Populorum Progressio,* 10, 41: *loc. cit.,* 262, 277-278.

[140] Cf. Benedict XVI, *Address to Members of the International Theological Commission,* 5th October 2007; *Address to the Participants in the International Congress on Natural Moral Law,* 12th February 2007.

60. In the search for solutions to the current economic crisis, *development aid for poor countries must be considered a valid means of creating wealth for all.* What aid programme is there that can hold out such significant growth prospects - even from the point of view of the world economy - as the support of populations that are still in the initial or early phases of economic development? From this perspective, more economically developed nations should do all they can to allocate larger portions of their gross domestic product to development aid, thus respecting the obligations that the international community has undertaken in this regard. One way of doing so is by reviewing their internal social assistance and welfare policies, applying the principle of subsidiarity and creating better integrated welfare systems, with the active participation of private individuals and civil society. In this way, it is actually possible to improve social services and welfare programmes, and at the same time to save resources - by eliminating waste and rejecting fraudulent claims - which could then be allocated to international solidarity. A more devolved and organic system of social solidarity, less bureaucratic but no less coordinated, would make it possible to harness much dormant energy, for the benefit of solidarity between peoples.

One possible approach to development aid would be to apply effectively what is known as fiscal subsidiarity, allowing citizens to decide how to allocate a portion of the taxes they pay to the State. Provided it does not degenerate into the promotion of special interests, this can help to stimulate forms of welfare solidarity from below, with obvious benefits in the area of solidarity for development as well.

61. Greater solidarity at the international level is seen especially in the ongoing promotion - even in the midst of economic crisis - of *greater access to education*, which is at the same time an essential precondition for effective international cooperation. The term "education" refers not only to classroom teaching and vocational training - both of which are important factors in development - but to the complete formation of the person. In this regard, there is a problem that should be highlighted: in order to educate, it is

necessary to know the nature of the human person, to know who he or she is. The increasing prominence of a relativistic understanding of that nature presents serious problems for education, especially moral education, jeopardising its universal extension. Yielding to this kind of relativism makes everyone poorer and has a negative impact on the effectiveness of aid to the most needy populations, who lack not only economic and technical means, but also educational methods and resources to assist people in realising their full human potential.

An illustration of the significance of this problem is offered by the phenomenon of *international tourism*,[141] which can be a major factor in economic development and cultural growth, but can also become an occasion for exploitation and moral degradation. The current situation offers unique opportunities for the economic aspects of development - that is to say the flow of money and the emergence of a significant amount of local enterprise - to be combined with the cultural aspects, chief among which is education. In many cases this is what happens, but in other cases international tourism has a negative educational impact both for the tourist and the local populace. The latter are often exposed to immoral or even perverted forms of conduct, as in the case of so-called sex tourism, to which many human beings are sacrificed even at a tender age. It is sad to note that this activity often takes place with the support of local governments, with silence from those in the tourists' countries of origin, and with the complicity of many of the tour operators. Even in less extreme cases, international tourism often follows a consumerist and hedonistic pattern, as a form of escapism planned in a manner typical of the countries of origin, and therefore not conducive to authentic encounter between persons and cultures. We need, therefore, to develop a different type of tourism that has the ability to promote genuine mutual understanding, without taking away from the element of rest and healthy recreation. Tourism of this type needs to increase, partly through closer coordination with the experience gained from international cooperation and enterprise for development.

---

[141] Cf. Benedict XVI, *Address to the Bishops of Thailand on their "Ad Limina" Visit,* 16th May 2008.

62. Another aspect of integral human development that is worthy of attention is the phenomenon of *migration*. This is a striking phenomenon because of the sheer numbers of people involved, the social, economic, political, cultural and religious problems it raises, and the dramatic challenges it poses to nations and the international community. We can say that we are facing a social phenomenon of epoch-making proportions that requires bold, forward-looking policies of international cooperation if it is to be handled effectively. Such policies should set out from close collaboration between the migrants' countries of origin and their countries of destination; it should be accompanied by adequate international norms able to coordinate different legislative systems with a view to safeguarding the needs and rights of individual migrants and their families, and at the same time, those of the host countries. No country can be expected to address today's problems of migration by itself. We are all witnesses of the burden of suffering, the dislocation and the aspirations that accompany the flow of migrants. The phenomenon, as everyone knows, is difficult to manage; but there is no doubt that foreign workers, despite any difficulties concerning integration, make a significant contribution to the economic development of the host country through their labour, besides that which they make to their country of origin through the money they send home. Obviously, these labourers cannot be considered as a commodity or a mere workforce. They must not, therefore, be treated like any other factor of production. Every migrant is a human person who, as such, possesses fundamental, inalienable rights that must be respected by everyone and in every circumstance.[142]

63. No consideration of the problems associated with development could fail to highlight the direct link between *poverty and unemployment*. In many cases, poverty results from a *violation of the dignity of human work*, either because work opportunities are limited (through unemployment or underemployment), or

---

[142] Cf. Pontifical Council for the Pastoral Care of Migrants and Itinerant People, Instruction *Erga Migrantes Caritas Christi* (3rd May 2004): *AAS* 96 (2004), 762-822.

"because a low value is put on work and the rights that flow from it, especially the right to a just wage and to the personal security of the worker and his or her family."[143] For this reason, on 1st May 2000 on the occasion of the Jubilee of Workers, my venerable predecessor Pope John Paul II issued an appeal for "a global coalition in favour of 'decent work'",[144] supporting the strategy of the International Labour Organisation. In this way, he gave a strong moral impetus to this objective, seeing it as an aspiration of families in every country of the world. What is meant by the word "decency" in regard to work? It means work that expresses the essential dignity of every man and woman in the context of their particular society: work that is freely chosen, effectively associating workers, both men and women, with the development of their community; work that enables the worker to be respected and free from any form of discrimination; work that makes it possible for families to meet their needs and provide schooling for their children, without the children themselves being forced into labour; work that permits the workers to organise themselves freely, and to make their voices heard; work that leaves enough room for rediscovering one's roots at a personal, familial and spiritual level; work that guarantees those who have retired a decent standard of living.

64. While reflecting on the theme of work, it is appropriate to recall how important it is that *labour unions* - which have always been encouraged and supported by the Church - should be open to the new perspectives that are emerging in the world of work. Looking to wider concerns than the specific category of labour for which they were formed, union organisations are called to address some of the new questions arising in our society: I am thinking, for example, of the complex of issues that social scientists describe in terms of a conflict between worker and consumer. Without necessarily endorsing the thesis that the central focus on the worker has given way to a central focus on the consumer, this would still

---

[143] John Paul II, Encyclical Letter *Laborem Exercens*, 8: *loc. cit.*, 594-598.

[144] Jubilee of Workers, *Greeting after Mass*, 1st May 2000.

appear to constitute new ground for unions to explore creatively. The global context in which work takes place also demands that national labour unions, which tend to limit themselves to defending the interests of their registered members, should turn their attention to those outside their membership, and in particular to workers in developing countries where social rights are often violated. The protection of these workers, partly achieved through appropriate initiatives aimed at their countries of origin, will enable trade unions to demonstrate the authentic ethical and cultural motivations that made it possible for them, in a different social and labour context, to play a decisive role in development. The Church's traditional teaching makes a valid distinction between the respective roles and functions of trade unions and politics. This distinction allows unions to identify civil society as the proper setting for their necessary activity of defending and promoting labour, especially on behalf of exploited and unrepresented workers, whose woeful condition is often ignored by the distracted eye of society.

65. *Finance*, therefore - through the renewed structures and operating methods that have to be designed after its misuse, which wreaked such havoc on the real economy - now needs to go back to being an *instrument directed towards improved wealth creation and development*. Insofar as they are instruments, the entire economy and finance, not just certain sectors, must be used in an ethical way so as to create suitable conditions for human development and for the development of peoples. It is certainly useful, and in some circumstances imperative, to launch financial initiatives in which the humanitarian dimension predominates. However, this must not obscure the fact that the entire financial system has to be aimed at sustaining true development. Above all, the intention to do good must not be considered incompatible with the effective capacity to produce goods. Financiers must rediscover the genuinely ethical foundation of their activity, so as not to abuse the sophisticated instruments which can serve to betray the interests of savers. Right intention, transparency, and the search for positive results are mutually compatible and must never be detached from one another.

If love is wise, it can find ways of working in accordance with provident and just expediency, as is illustrated in a significant way by much of the experience of credit unions.

Both the regulation of the financial sector, so as to safeguard weaker parties and discourage scandalous speculation, and experimentation with new forms of finance, designed to support development projects, are positive experiences that should be further explored and encouraged, highlighting *the responsibility of the investor*. Furthermore, the *experience of micro-finance,* which has its roots in the thinking and activity of the civil humanists - I am thinking especially of the birth of pawnbroking - should be strengthened and fine-tuned. This is all the more necessary in these days when financial difficulties can become severe for many of the more vulnerable sectors of the population, who should be protected from the risk of usury and from despair. The weakest members of society should be helped to defend themselves against usury, just as poor peoples should be helped to derive real benefit from micro-credit, in order to discourage the exploitation that is possible in these two areas. Since rich countries are also experiencing new forms of poverty, micro-finance can give practical assistance by launching new initiatives and opening up new sectors for the benefit of the weaker elements in society, even at a time of general economic downturn.

66. Global interconnectedness has led to the emergence of a new political power, that of *consumers and their associations*. This is a phenomenon that needs to be further explored, as it contains positive elements to be encouraged as well as excesses to be avoided. It is good for people to realise that purchasing is always a moral - and not simply economic - act. Hence *the consumer has a specific social responsibility*, which goes hand-in-hand with the social responsibility of the enterprise. Consumers should be continually educated[145] regarding their daily role, which can be exercised with respect for moral principles without diminishing the intrinsic

---

[145] Cf. John Paul II, Encyclical Letter *Centesimus Annus*, 36: *loc. cit.*, 838-840.

economic rationality of the act of purchasing. In the retail industry, particularly at times like the present when purchasing power has diminished and people must live more frugally, it is necessary to explore other paths: for example, forms of cooperative purchasing like the consumer cooperatives that have been in operation since the nineteenth century, partly through the initiative of Catholics. In addition, it can be helpful to promote new ways of marketing products from deprived areas of the world, so as to guarantee their producers a decent return. However, certain conditions need to be met: the market should be genuinely transparent; the producers, as well as increasing their profit margins, should also receive improved formation in professional skills and technology; and finally, trade of this kind must not become hostage to partisan ideologies. A more incisive role for consumers, as long as they themselves are not manipulated by associations that do not truly represent them, is a desirable element for building economic democracy.

67. In the face of the unrelenting growth of global interdependence, there is a strongly felt need, even in the midst of a global recession, for a reform of the *United Nations Organisation*, and likewise of *economic institutions and international finance*, so that the concept of the family of nations can acquire real teeth. One also senses the urgent need to find innovative ways of implementing the principle of the *responsibility to protect*[146] *and of giving poorer nations an effective voice in shared decision-making. This seems necessary in order to arrive at a political, juridical and economic order which can increase and give direction to international cooperation for the development of all peoples in solidarity. To manage the global economy; to revive economies hit by the crisis; to avoid any deterioration of the present crisis and the greater imbalances that would result; to bring about integral and timely disarmament, food security and peace; to guarantee the protection of the environment and to regulate migration: for all this, there is urgent need of a*

---

[146] Cf. Benedict XVI, *Address to the Members of the General Assembly of the United Nations Organisation*, New York, 18th April 2008.

true world political authority, as my predecessor Blessed John XXIII indicated some years ago. Such an authority would need to be regulated by law, to observe consistently the principles of subsidiarity and solidarity, to seek to establish the common good,[147] and *to make a commitment to securing authentic integral human development inspired by the values of charity in truth.* Furthermore, such an authority would need to be universally recognised and to be vested with the effective power to ensure security for all, regard for justice, and respect for rights.[148] Obviously it would have to have the authority to ensure compliance with its decisions from all parties, and also with the coordinated measures adopted in various international forums. Without this, despite the great progress accomplished in various sectors, international law would risk being conditioned by the balance of power among the strongest nations. The integral development of peoples and international cooperation require the establishment of a greater degree of international ordering, marked by subsidiarity, for the management of globalisation.[149] They also require the construction of a social order that at last conforms to the moral order, to the interconnection between moral and social spheres, and to the link between politics and the economic and civil spheres, as envisaged by the Charter of the United Nations.

---

[147] Cf. John XXIII, Encyclical Letter *Pacem in Terris, loc. cit.,* 293; Pontifical Council for Justice and Peace, *Compendium of the Social Doctrine of the Church,* 441.

[148] Cf. Second Vatican Ecumenical Council, Pastoral Constitution on the Church in the Modern World, *Gaudium et Spes,* 82.

[149] Cf. John Paul II, Encyclical Letter *Sollicitudo Rei Socialis,* 43: *loc. cit.,* 574-575.

CHAPTER SIX

THE DEVELOPMENT OF PEOPLES AND TECHNOLOGY

68. The development of peoples is intimately linked to the development of individuals. The human person by nature is actively involved in his own development. The development in question is not simply the result of natural mechanisms, since as everybody knows, we are all capable of making free and responsible choices. Nor is it merely at the mercy of our caprice, since we all know that we are a gift, not something self-generated. Our freedom is profoundly shaped by our being, and by its limits. No one shapes his own conscience arbitrarily, but we all build our own "I" on the basis of a "self" which is given to us. Not only are other persons outside our control, but each one of us is outside his or her own control. *A person's development is compromised, if he claims to be solely responsible for producing what he becomes.* By analogy, the development of peoples goes awry if humanity thinks it can re-create itself through the "wonders" of technology, just as economic development is exposed as a destructive sham if it relies on the "wonders" of finance in order to sustain unnatural and consumerist growth. In the face of such Promethean presumption, we must fortify our love for a freedom that is not merely arbitrary, but is rendered truly human by acknowledgment of the good that underlies it. To this end, man needs to look inside himself in order to recognise the fundamental norms of the natural moral law which God has written on our hearts.

69. The challenge of development today is closely linked to *technological progress*, with its astounding applications in the field of biology. Technology - it is worth emphasizing - is a profoundly human reality, linked to the autonomy and freedom of man. In technology we express and confirm the hegemony of the spirit over matter. "The human spirit, 'increasingly free of its bondage to creatures, can be more easily drawn to the worship

and contemplation of the Creator'."[150] Technology enables us to exercise dominion over matter, to reduce risks, to save labour, to improve our conditions of life. It touches the heart of the vocation of human labour: in technology, seen as the product of his genius, man recognizes himself and forges his own humanity. Technology is the objective side of human action[151] whose origin and *raison d'etre* is found in the subjective element: the worker himself. For this reason, technology is never merely technology. It reveals man and his aspirations towards development, it expresses the inner tension that impels him gradually to overcome material limitations. *Technology, in this sense, is a response to God's command to till and to keep the land* (cf. *Gn* 2:15) that he has entrusted to humanity, and it must serve to reinforce the covenant between human beings and the environment, a covenant that should mirror God's creative love.

70. Technological development can give rise to the idea that technology is self-sufficient when too much attention is given to the *"how"* questions, and not enough to the many *"why"* questions underlying human activity. For this reason technology can appear ambivalent. Produced through human creativity as a tool of personal freedom, technology can be understood as a manifestation of absolute freedom, the freedom that seeks to prescind from the limits inherent in things. The process of globalisation could replace ideologies with technology,[152] allowing the latter to become an ideological power that threatens to confine us within an *a priori* that holds us back from encountering being and truth. Were that to happen, we would all know, evaluate and make decisions about our life situations from within a technocratic cultural perspective to which we would belong structurally, without ever being able to discover a meaning that is not of our own making. The "technical"

---

[150] Paul VI, Encyclical Letter *Populorum Progressio*, 41: loc. cit., 277-278; cf. Second Vatican Ecumenical Council, Pastoral Constitution on the Church in the Modern World *Gaudium et Spes*, 57.

[151] Cf. John Paul II, Encyclical Letter *Laborem Exercens*, 5: loc. cit., 586-589.

[152] Cf. Paul VI, Apostolic Letter *Octogesima Adveniens*, 29: loc. cit., 420.

worldview that follows from this vision is now so dominant that truth has come to be seen as coinciding with the possible. But when the sole criterion of truth is efficiency and utility, development is automatically denied. True development does not consist primarily in "doing". The key to development is a mind capable of thinking in technological terms and grasping the fully human meaning of human activities, within the context of the holistic meaning of the individual's being. Even when we work through satellites or through remote electronic impulses, our actions always remain human, an expression of our responsible freedom. Technology is highly attractive because it draws us out of our physical limitations and broadens our horizon. *But human freedom is authentic only when it responds to the fascination of technology with decisions that are the fruit of moral responsibility.* Hence the pressing need for formation in an ethically responsible use of technology. Moving beyond the fascination that technology exerts, we must reappropriate the true meaning of freedom, which is not an intoxication with total autonomy, but a response to the call of being, beginning with our own personal being.

71. This deviation from solid humanistic principles that a technical mindset can produce is seen today in certain technological applications in the fields of development and peace. Often the development of peoples is considered a matter of financial engineering, the freeing up of markets, the removal of tariffs, investment in production, and institutional reforms - in other words, a purely technical matter. All these factors are of great importance, but we have to ask why technical choices made thus far have yielded rather mixed results. We need to think hard about the cause. Development will never be fully guaranteed through automatic or impersonal forces, whether they derive from the market or from international politics. *Development is impossible without upright men and women, without financiers and politicians whose consciences are finely attuned to the requirements of the common good.* Both professional competence and moral consistency are necessary. When technology is allowed to take over, the result is

187

confusion between ends and means, such that the sole criterion for action in business is thought to be the maximisation of profit, in politics the consolidation of power, and in science the findings of research. Often, underneath the intricacies of economic, financial and political interconnections, there remain misunderstandings, hardships and injustice. The flow of technological know-how increases, but it is those in possession of it who benefit, while the situation on the ground for the peoples who live in its shadow remains unchanged: for them there is little chance of emancipation.

72. Even peace can run the risk of being considered a technical product, merely the outcome of agreements between governments or of initiatives aimed at ensuring effective economic aid. It is true that *peace-building* requires the constant interplay of diplomatic contacts, economic, technological and cultural exchanges, agreements on common projects, as well as joint strategies to curb the threat of military conflict and to root out the underlying causes of terrorism. Nevertheless, if such efforts are to have lasting effects, they must be based on values rooted in the truth of human life. That is, the voice of the peoples affected must be heard and their situation must be taken into consideration, if their expectations are to be correctly interpreted. One must align oneself, so to speak, with the unsung efforts of so many individuals deeply committed to bringing peoples together and to facilitating development on the basis of love and mutual understanding. Among them are members of the Christian faithful, involved in the great task of upholding the fully human dimension of development and peace.

73. Linked to technological development is the increasingly pervasive presence of the *means of social communications*. It is almost impossible today to imagine the life of the human family without them. For better or for worse, they are so integral a part of life today that it seems quite absurd to maintain that they are neutral - and hence unaffected by any moral considerations concerning people. Often such views, stressing the strictly technical nature of the media, effectively support their subordination to economic

interests intent on dominating the market and, not least, to attempts to impose cultural models that serve ideological and political agendas. Given the media's fundamental importance in engineering changes in attitude towards reality and the human person, we must reflect carefully on their influence, especially in regard to the ethical-cultural dimension of globalisation and the development of peoples in solidarity. Mirroring what is required for an ethical approach to globalisation and development, so too the *meaning and purpose of the media must be sought within an anthropological perspective.* This means that they can have a *civilising effect* not only when, thanks to technological development, they increase the possibilities of communicating information, but above all when they are geared towards a vision of the person and the common good that reflects truly universal values. Just because social communications increase the possibilities of interconnection and the dissemination of ideas, it does not follow that they promote freedom or internationalise development and democracy for all. To achieve goals of this kind, they need to focus on promoting the dignity of persons and peoples, they need to be clearly inspired by charity and placed at the service of truth, of the good, and of natural and supernatural fraternity. In fact, human freedom is intrinsically linked with these higher values. The media can make an important contribution towards the growth in communion of the human family and the *ethos* of society when they are used to promote universal participation in the common search for what is just.

74. A particularly crucial battleground in today's cultural struggle between the supremacy of technology and human moral responsibility is the field of *bioethics*, where the very possibility of integral human development is radically called into question. In this most delicate and critical area, the fundamental question asserts itself force-fully: is man the product of his own labours or does he depend on God? Scientific discoveries in this field and the possibilities of technological intervention seem so advanced as to force a choice between two types of reasoning: reason open to transcendence or reason closed within immanence. We are presented

189

with a clear *either/or*. Yet the rationality of a self-centred use of technology proves to be irrational because it implies a decisive rejection of meaning and value. It is no coincidence that closing the door to transcendence brings one up short against a difficulty: how could being emerge from nothing, how could intelligence be born from chance?[153] Faced with these dramatic questions, reason and faith can come to each other's assistance. Only together will they save man. *Entranced by an exclusive reliance on technology, reason without faith is doomed to flounder in an illusion of its own omnipotence. Faith without reason risks being cut off from everyday life.*[154]

75. Paul VI had already recognised and drawn attention to the global dimension of the social question.[155] Following his lead, we need to affirm today that *the social question has become a radically anthropological question*, in the sense that it concerns not just how life is conceived but also how it is manipulated, as bio-technology places it increasingly under man's control. *In vitro* fertilisation, embryo research, the possibility of manufacturing clones and human hybrids: all this is now emerging and being promoted in today's highly disillusioned culture, which believes it has mastered every mystery, because the origin of life is now within our grasp. Here we see the clearest expression of technology's supremacy. In this type of culture, the conscience is simply invited to take note of technological possibilities. Yet we must not underestimate the disturbing scenarios that threaten our future, or the powerful new instruments that the "culture of death" has at its disposal. To the tragic and widespread scourge of abortion we may well have to add in the future - indeed it is already surreptitiously present - the systematic eugenic programming of births. At the other end of

[153] Cf. Benedict XVI, *Address to the Participants in the Fourth National Congress of the Church in Italy*, Verona, 19th October 2006; Id., *Homily at Mass*, Islinger Feld, Regensburg, 12th September 2006.

[154] Cf. Congregation for the Doctrine of the Faith, Instruction on certain bioethical questions *Dignitas Personae* (8th September 2008): *AAS* 100 (2008), 858-887.

[155] Cf. Encyclical Letter *Populorum Progressio*, 3: *loc. cit.*, 258.

the spectrum, a pro-euthanasia mindset is making inroads as an equally damaging assertion of control over life that under certain circumstances is deemed no longer worth living. Underlying these scenarios are cultural viewpoints that deny human dignity. These practices in turn foster a materialistic and mechanistic understanding of human life. Who could measure the negative effects of this kind of mentality for development? How can we be surprised by the indifference shown towards situations of human degradation, when such indifference extends even to our attitude towards what is and is not human? What is astonishing is the arbitrary and selective determination of what to put forward today as worthy of respect. Insignificant matters are considered shocking, yet unprecedented injustices seem to be widely tolerated. While the poor of the world continue knocking on the doors of the rich, the world of affluence runs the risk of no longer hearing those knocks, on account of a conscience that can no longer distinguish what is human. God reveals man to himself; reason and faith work hand in hand to demonstrate to us what is good, provided we want to see it; the natural law, in which creative Reason shines forth, reveals our greatness, but also our wretchedness insofar as we fail to recognise the call to moral truth.

76. One aspect of the contemporary technological mindset is the tendency to consider the problems and emotions of the interior life from a purely psychological point of view, even to the point of neurological reductionism. In this way man's interiority is emptied of its meaning and gradually our awareness of the human soul's ontological depths, as probed by the saints, is lost. *The question of development is closely bound up with our understanding of the human soul,* insofar as we often reduce the self to the psyche and confuse the soul's health with emotional well-being. These over-simplifications stem from a profound failure to understand the spiritual life, and they obscure the fact that the development of individuals and peoples depends partly on the resolution of problems of a spiritual nature. *Development must include not just material growth but also spiritual growth,* since the human person

is a "unity of body and soul",[156] born of God's creative love and destined for eternal life. The human being develops when he grows in the spirit, when his soul comes to know itself and the truths that God has implanted deep within, when he enters into dialogue with himself and his Creator. When he is far away from God, man is unsettled and ill at ease. Social and psychological alienation and the many neuroses that afflict affluent societies are attributable in part to spiritual factors. A prosperous society, highly developed in material terms but weighing heavily on the soul, is not of itself conducive to authentic development. The new forms of slavery to drugs and the lack of hope into which so many people fall can be explained not only in sociological and psychological terms but also in essentially spiritual terms. The emptiness in which the soul feels abandoned, despite the availability of countless therapies for body and psyche, leads to suffering. *There cannot be holistic development and universal common good unless people's spiritual and moral welfare is taken into account*, considered in their totality as body and soul.

77. The supremacy of technology tends to prevent people from recognising anything that cannot be explained in terms of matter alone. Yet everyone experiences the many immaterial and spiritual dimensions of life. Knowing is not simply a material act, since the object that is known always conceals something beyond the empirical datum. All our knowledge, even the most simple, is always a minor miracle, since it can never be fully explained by the material instruments that we apply to it. In every truth there is something more than we would have expected, in the love that we receive there is always an element that surprises us. We should never cease to marvel at these things. In all knowledge and in every act of love the human soul experiences something "over and above", which seems very much like a gift that we receive, or a height to which we are raised. The development of individuals

---

[156] Second Vatican Ecumenical Council, Pastoral Constitution on the Church in the Modern World *Gaudium et Spes*, 14.

and peoples is likewise located on a height, if we consider *the spiritual dimension* that must be present if such development is to be authentic. It requires new eyes and a new heart, capable of *rising above a materialistic vision of human events*, capable of glimpsing in development the "beyond" that technology cannot give. By following this path, it is possible to pursue the integral human development that takes its direction from the driving force of charity in truth.

CONCLUSION

78. Without God man neither knows which way to go, nor even understands who he is. In the face of the enormous problems surrounding the development of peoples, which almost make us yield to discouragement, we find solace in the sayings of our Lord Jesus Christ, who teaches us: "Apart from me you can do nothing" (*Jn* 15:5) and then encourages us: "I am with you always, to the close of the age" (*Mt* 28:20). As we contemplate the vast amount of work to be done, we are sustained by our faith that God is present alongside those who come together in his name to work for justice. Paul VI recalled in *Populorum Progressio* that man cannot bring about his own progress unaided, because by himself he cannot establish an authentic humanism. Only if we are aware of our calling, as individuals and as a community, to be part of God's family as his sons and daughters, will we be able to generate a new vision and muster new energy in the service of a truly integral humanism. The greatest service to development, then, is a Christian humanism[157] that enkindles charity and takes its lead from truth, accepting both as a lasting gift from God. Openness to God makes us open towards our brothers and sisters and towards an understanding of life as a joyful task to be accomplished in a spirit of solidarity. On the other hand, ideological rejection of God and an atheism of indifference, oblivious to the Creator and at risk of becoming equally oblivious to human values, constitute some of the chief obstacles to development today. *A humanism which excludes God is an inhuman humanism.* Only a humanism open to the Absolute can guide us in the promotion and building of forms of social and civic life - structures, institutions, culture and *ethos* - without exposing us to the risk of becoming ensnared by the fashions of the moment. Awareness of God's undying love sustains us in our laborious and stimulating work for justice and the development of peoples, amid successes and failures, in the ceaseless pursuit of a just ordering of human affairs. *God's love*

---

[157] Cf. Paul VI, Encyclical Letter *Populorum Progressio*, 42: *loc. cit.*, 278.

calls us to move beyond the limited and the ephemeral, it gives us the courage to continue seeking and working for the benefit of all, even if this cannot be achieved immediately and if what we are able to achieve, alongside political authorities and those working in the field of economics, is always less than we might wish.[158] God gives us the strength to fight and to suffer for love of the common good, because he is our All, our greatest hope.

79. *Development needs Christians with their arms raised towards God* in prayer, Christians moved by the knowledge that truth-filled love, *caritas in veritate,* from which authentic development proceeds, is not produced by us, but given to us. For this reason, even in the most difficult and complex times, besides recognising what is happening, we must above all else turn to God's love. Development requires attention to the spiritual life, a serious consideration of the experiences of trust in God, spiritual fellowship in Christ, reliance upon God's providence and mercy, love and forgiveness, self-denial, acceptance of others, justice and peace. All this is essential if "hearts of stone" are to be transformed into "hearts of flesh" (*Ezk* 36:26), rendering life on earth "divine" and thus more worthy of humanity. All this is *of man,* because man is the subject of his own existence; and at the same time it is *of God,* because God is at the beginning and end of all that is good, all that leads to salvation: "the world or life or death or the present or the future, all are yours; and you are Christ's; and Christ is God's" (1 *Co* 3:22-23). Christians long for the entire human family to call upon God as "Our Father!" In union with the only-begotten Son, may all people learn to pray to the Father and to ask him, in the words that Jesus himself taught us, for the grace to glorify him by living according to his will, to receive the daily bread that we need, to be understanding and generous towards our debtors, not to be tempted beyond our limits, and to be delivered from evil (cf. *Mt* 6:9-13).

At the conclusion of the *Pauline Year,* I gladly express this hope in the Apostle's own words, taken from the *Letter to the Romans*:

---

158 Cf. Benedict XVI, Encyclical Letter *Spe Salvi,* 35: *loc. cit.,* 1013-1014.

"Let love be genuine; hate what is evil, hold fast to what is good; love one another with brotherly affection; outdo one another in showing honour" (*Rm* 12:9-10). May the Virgin Mary - proclaimed *Mater Ecclesiae* by Paul VI and honoured by Christians as *Speculum Iustitiae* and *Regina Pacis* - protect us and obtain for us, through her heavenly intercession, the strength, hope and joy necessary to continue to dedicate ourselves with generosity to the task of bringing about the *"development of the whole man and of all men"*.[159]

Given in Rome, at Saint Peter's, on 29th June, the Solemnity of the Holy Apostles Peter and Paul, in the year 2009, the fifth of my Pontificate.

BENEDICT PP. XVI

---

[159] Paul VI, Encyclical Letter *Populorum Progressio*, 42: *loc. cit.*, 278.

INDEX

References to footnotes are indicated by *n* after the page number (e.g. *42n*)
Books of the Bible are found under their individual names (e.g. *Genesis, Timothy 1* etc.)

J

Jesus Christ 7, 10, 13, 20-2, 25,
27, 42, 47, 51, 58, 60, 68, 73,
80, 92, 102, 120, 195;
on the Cross 103;
and judgement 99;
parables of Jesus 97;
teaching of 107
Job: 23:3 47;
23:5-6 45;
23:15-16 47
John: 1:14 102;
1:29 89;
1:51 15;
2:4 50;
3:16 7, 27;
4:10 7;
4:16 7;
7:37-38 15;
7:38 51;
7:38-39 27;
8:22 107;
8:32 114;
10:10 80;
12:25 13;
13:1 27, 50, 80, 109;
13:1-13 27;
14:6 107;
14:9 23;
14:27 103;
15:5 195;
15:13 27;
16:22 68;
16:33 103;
17:3 80;
17:22 171;
19:25-27 51;
19:26 103;

19:27 51;
19:30 27, 80;
19:37 20, 27;
20:22 27
John 1 85;
2:1 100;
3:18 111;
4:8 20, 42;
4:8,16 107-8;
4:9 23;
4:10 23;
4:20 23

John Bosco, Saint 49

John of God, Saint 49

John Paul II, Pope: canonisation
of St Josephine Bakhita 56;
*Address to the Civil Authorities
etc of Austria* 169*n*;
*Address to the Pontifical
Academies of Theology and of
St Thomas Aquinas* 172*n*;
*Address to the Pontifical
Academy of Social Sciences* 154;
Address to the United Nations
133*n*;
*Address to the Vatican
Foundation "Centesimus
Annus - Pro Pontifice"* 169*n*;
Centesimus Annus 33, 114*n*,
117*n*, 120*n*, 121*n*, 123*n*, 130,
133*n*, 139, 143*n*, 145, 148, 151*n*,
152*n*, 167, 169*n*, 173, 174*n*, 182*n*;
Christifideles Laici 37, 39*n*;
Evangelium Vitae 119, 135*n*,
169*n*;
Fides et Ratio 139*n*;
Laborem Exercens 33, 117*n*,
152, 180, 186*n*;

S

Saints, and charity 49-51

Sallust, *De coniuratione Catilinae* 24

salvation 55, 66, 69-71, 79, 80, 88, 94, 99-100, 101, 196

sarcophagi, early Christian 60-1

science: and the Church's social doctrine 139-40;
as a substitute for faith 71-2, 74, 79

Second Vatican Council 34, 38, 111*n*, 115, 117

secularism 46, 173

Severus, Sulpicius, *Vita Sancti Martini* 49*n*

sex education 158

sex tourism 178

sexuality 12, 119, 158-9, 168

Shema 16

shepherd, Jesus Christ as 60, 61, 64

Simeon 102

slavery 56-7, 58-9

social communication, and technology 188-9

social inequality 128-30, 140, 154

social justice 32-3, 131, 145

social security 131-2

Song of Songs 12-13, 18

soul, human 11-12, 71, 97, 100-1, 137, 144, 191-2

spiritual life 191-3, 196

State, the: relationship with the Church 34-7, 39, 114;
responsibilities of 153

subsidiarity 32, 36, 162, 174-5, 177, 184

suffering: and charity 28, 30, 36, 38;
and faith 87, 88-92, 94-5;
and Job 47;
and Saint Augustine 47;
of souls 100;
spiritual 42, 132, 192

syncretism, religious 171-2

T

technology, and human development 118-19, 185-93

Teresa of Calcutta, Blessed ('Mother Teresa') 25, 46, 49

terrorism 137, 188

Tertullian, Apologeticum 29-30

Thessalonians 1: 3:2 88; 4:13 56

Thomas Aquinas, Saint, *Summa Theologiae* 62, 170*n*

Thuan, Cardinal Nguyen Van: *Prayers of Hope* 85; *Testimony of Hope* 86

Timothy 1: 1:5 69; 2:6 80

Timothy 2: 1:7 65

Titus: 3:4 47

Torah 17

tourism, international 178

trade union organisations 132, 180-1

Trinity, the 27, 170-1